THE LANDSCAPE QUILT

by
Sheryl
Morrow
Robinson

BOYD PUBLISHING

P. O. Box 6753
Wheeling, WV 26003

Acknowledgments

Photography by Catherine McConnell Stanton, Pittsburgh, PA.
Graphic Design and Layout by SPPS, Fountain Valley, CA.
Printed in Hong Kong.

With Special Thanks to:

Pat Altmyer, for encouraging me to begin this project;

B. J. Elvgren, whose quilts have always inspired me;

Lynn Morrow Stiles, who taught me computer literacy;

D. Michaeline Reed and Lisa Sauer, for the use of their quilts;

Catherine McConnell Stanton, for the photography;

Sam Newbury, for the use of his photographic equipment;

Dot Schachter, for proofreading;

Virginia Morrow Folks, for her encouragement and advice;

my Wednesday night group, Quilter's Triangle, for their support and friendship;

and my husband, Alan, and my son, Elliott, for their tolerance and sense of humor.

ISBN:1-879844-07-9.

For my grandmothers
Rose Apel Morrow
and
Antonina Zuffante Bler
and my mother
Virginia Bler Morrow Folks
who have shaped my life and values
by their strength and Christian beliefs.

TABLE OF CONTENTS

FOREWORD

The landscape quilt artist depicts the countryside she views around her. She wants to evoke the mood of the moment that she has experienced, whether it is the feeling of peace and contentment of the newly fallen snow, the excitement and energy of a rapidly flowing stream, or the solitude and loneliness of the desert.

Most often it is either a familiar site that she has visited or a place that she longs to visit. She may be inspired by a drive down a long winding road, the rocks along the shore, the changing autumn leaves, the ocean waves beating against the shore, or a remote mountain village.

It is not only the country scene that the quilt artist desires to create but also the cityscape. Lucretia Romey, Louise Silk, and B.J. Elvgren are quilt artists who capture the essence of the urban scene such as skyscrapers, neighborhoods, parks, playgrounds and cliffside homes. Rhoda Cohen, Risë Nagin, and Judi Warren have designed windowscape quilts – quilts in which a window frames the exterior view.

All elements of nature call out to the quilter to be represented in a quilt. The quilt artist must decide if her design is to portray nature in a realistic or in an abstract manner. Not only is this virtually impossible to do, but it does not permit her creative spirit to emerge. She must decide whether to express her reaction to the scene or simply to recreate the site. She chooses the moment in time – winter, spring, summer, or fall – as well as the degree of light – sunlight, moonlight, dusk, or dawn.

It is her option to change the landscape by eliminating, by adding or by rearranging the various elements of the natural scene to define her intended mood. To create a sense of solitude, she may eliminate houses; to create energy and movement within the landscape, she may add children and animals; to create a harmonious scene, she may rearrange the components of the landscape. Each change that the quilter makes enables her to become more creative and intuitive.

CHAPTER ONE

FROM INSPIRATION TO DESIGN

Words are my first source of inspiration. Many times a single word suggests a quilt subject. One afternoon, the word landslide sparked my imagination; several days later, I spotted a bulldozer atop a hill. I rushed home to get the camera and returned to take a roll of photographs of the hillside and the rocks piled at the bottom. These photographs led me to design and make a three-dimensional quilt that depicted the hill that had been bulldozed. Make lists of nouns that suggest landscapes, seasons and weather conditions:

old road	meadows	rain storm	lake
bridge	cornfields	lightning	river
mill	prairie	dark clouds	waterfall
barn	sand dunes	sunset	pond
fence	beaches	snowfall	stream
farm house	mountains	fog	puddle

Does this list of nouns spark your imagination? I envision a scene in which the old road is a rutted, muddy lane that curves through cornfields; it disappears in the fields and then reappears at the farm buildings. The sky is filled with dark, threatening storm clouds, the wind is bending the tree branches, and the sheep are returning to the barn.

At this point, the quilt designer is ready to do one of the following two steps: sketch or search. For the quilter who has the ability to draw, the next step is to make a sketch which includes the list of words. For the quilter who feels that she does not have the skills necessary to sketch this scene, her search for photographs which include the list of words begins.

Always begin with a scene that is familiar and pleasing to you. This does not mean that the scene has to be pretty. You may choose to illustrate a cityscape of a run-down neighborhood or of steel mills. Neither of these subjects is lovely, yet either will elicit a response from you and from the viewer.

Search for photographs of landscapes in the Sierra Club and Audubon calendars; in greeting cards; in photography books by such noted photographers as Eliot Porter and Ansel Adams; in nature books; in library slides; in magazines such as *Country Living, Art in America, and Southwestern Art;* in books on landscape paintings; and in your collection of vacation photos. Keep all these photos, sketches and magazine clippings in a folder or notebook. Include detailed pictures of doors, buildings, fences and animals.

The most difficult source of inspiration to use is the photograph of a painted landscape. The painter, in expressing his reaction to the scene, has either included or omitted details; the quilt designer is then responding to her impression of the painting and not to the original location itself. When using a photograph as the idea source, the quilter has the options to include as much or as little of the detail as she desires and to determine the season, the time of day and the weather conditions.

Keep graph paper with you as you leaf through art books and magazines. Paintings by artists Charles Wysockie, Grandma Moses and Jane Wooster provide an abundance of ideas for buildings. When you find a pleasing subject such as a house or barn, sketch a simplified outline of the building onto graph paper. Place these sketches into your file folder. At a later date, these sketches may be combined into an original composition or may be enlarged on a copier machine to include into your selected scene.

If the landscape is a local scene, your camera becomes your design tool. It will record the setting and perspective, provide infinite detail, capture the patterns of light and shadow and note the weather conditions. Take your camera to the location and stand to the far right; snap a photo; move one step to the left; take another photo; move to the left again. Continue this procedure until you have photographed the scene from right to left. Repeat this procedure, photographing from a lower or higher angle. Because the camera can record the most data in the shortest amount of time, take close-up photos of plants, leaves, doorways, and windows. Photographing your scene at different hours permits the camera to record the various effects of light on the scene.

Jot down some notes about the scene – was the wind blowing, did you hear human voices, animal sounds or traffic noise? If so, you may wish to include people or animals into your scene and to quilt in the wind lines.

Because nature provides infinite details, it is impossible to record every rock and pebble or tree and flower. In order to assist you in eliminating detail from the scene or in determining the perfect composition, make a viewfinder or window template:

1. Cut a window template from black construction paper or cardboard. The window space should be about 2" x 2" or 2" x 3" and the frame should be about 2" wide.

2. Move the window template over the photograph. Look through the window, and focus on only one area at a time.

3. The closer the window template is held to the photograph, the smaller the view will be. The further the window template is held from the photograph, the larger the view will be.

4. You can now decide whether to include the entire scene or to focus on one section of it and whether to emphasize the vertical or horizontal format.

As you view your photos, ask yourself the following questions:

1. What did I first notice? Was it the shape of the hills against the skyline or the cluster of farm buildings or the colors?

2. What is the focal point? To what place do my eyes repeatedly return?

3. What is the relationship between the focal point and the other objects?

4. Are there any signs of human or animal life? Is there movement?

5. Are the edges of buildings straight and parallel or sagging and bowed?

Once you have studied the photo for factual information, view it again with a creative eye. The landscape scene is not intended to be an exact copy of nature, but rather an expression of your feelings. Do you want it to evoke peacefulness and serenity or restlessness and agitation? If you have been using the work of a noted painter or photographer, you must make every effort to modify, alter or rearrange the original material. What changes are needed to express your feelings? To create your personal statement or response to the scene, I recommend that you execute at least three of the sixteen suggestions from the list on the following page.

SUGGESTIONS

1. Exaggerate or distort the subject by using a photograph that is out of focus.

2. Reposition objects to create varied spaces.

3. Focus on only one section of the scene.

4. Change the amount of foreground (fields) or background (sky). Either enlarge or decrease.

5. Eliminate an object (perhaps trees) or include more.

6. Break the border. Carry an element from the interior of the quilt over the border. Example: Branches of a tree, a fence or a path.

7. Change warm colors to cool colors.

8. Use black and white photos so that there is no color to influence you; there are only values of black and white.

9. Change the value of the colors.

10. Change the season.

11. Make three-dimensional rocks, flowers or bushes.

12. Use paint to create details, shadow and dimension.

13. Embellish with beads, found objects and embroidery.

14. Combine views from two or three photographs to yield a postcard style scene.

15. Combine photos of the same object viewed from three angles or three different distances.

16. Give credit to the original artist.

MATERIALS LIST

photographs, pictures
file folder or notebook
17" x 22" graph paper
tracing paper
mechanical pencil
18" ruler, clear plastic
Scotch tape
masking tape
Sharpie® pen, black
white Thermolam
fabric
fabric scissors
100% cotton thread

John James needles
pins
sewing machine
embroidery thread
beads
beading needles
Nemo beading thread
acrylic paints
paint brushes
quilt marking pencils
quilting needles
batting

1. Tape a photograph or picture to the table top. As an example, assume we are working with a photograph of an old mill.

2. Tape a piece of tracing paper over the photograph. The tracing paper must be large enough to cover the original photograph.

3. Draw an outline around the photograph. This will determine whether the quilt's shape is to be square or rectangular.

4. Trace as much of the photograph as possible. Add details such as doorways and shutters. Including more details in the preliminary tracing makes it easier to transpose them to the full-size cartoon. Refer to Illustration 1.1 below.

Illus. 1.1a. Graphic to be made into a quilt (e.g., a photograph.)

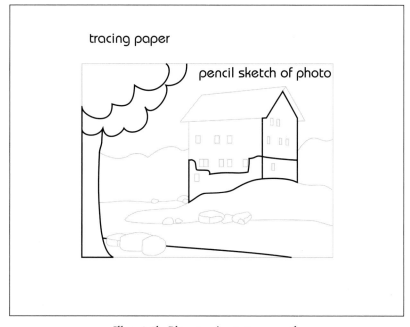

tracing paper

pencil sketch of photo

Illus. 1.1b. Place tracing paper over the photograph, then pencil sketch the designs.

5. Remove the tracing paper from atop the photograph and place the tracing paper onto graph paper that has been ruled into four squares per inch. For example, ¼" blue line quadrille paper.

6. Position the tracing onto the graph paper so that at least two sides of the tracing are lined up with the blue lines on the graph paper.

7. Number the squares on the graph paper from left to right across the upper horizontal line of the rectangle. Number the squares from top to bottom on the left hand margin. The number of squares in each direction will determine the size of the quilt scene. Example: Our scene measures 24 squares horizontally by 18 squares vertically. If each square were to represent 1", our design would measure 24" x 18". If each square were to represent 1½", the design area would measure 36" x 27". Two inch squares equal 48" x 36", 2½" squares equal 60" x 45", and 3" squares equal 72" x 54". The available wall space will determine the ratio and measurement you select. For the beginning landscape designer, the 36" x 27" or the 48" x 36" format is sufficient. With an addition of 8" borders, the finished size would be either 44" x 35" or 56" x 44".

8. Using large sheets of paper (such as graph paper or tracing paper), tape together enough sheets to equal the interior design area plus 2" on each side.

9. Using a ruler and black Sharpie® pen, draw a rectangle 36" x 27". This rectangle becomes the full-size drawing or cartoon.

10. Because we chose the ratio of 1 square equals 1½" for our example, we must now make a mark every 1½" around the perimeter of the cartoon. If you are using graph paper, it is not necessary to connect the vertical and horizontal lines. If you are using unruled paper such as butcher's paper, it is advisable to rule the paper into 1½" squares.

11. Number the squares on the graph paper across the top and down the left side of the cartoon in the same manner as you labeled the graph paper under the tracing.

12. Transpose all lines from the tracing onto the full-size cartoon. Illustration 1.2 demonstrates the following points to draw the mill:

    a. Begin with the straight lines which are the vertical

b. Determine the beginning and end points of these vertical lines. Mark these points on the cartoon.

c. Using a ruler and mechanical pencil, draw the vertical lines by connecting the points.

d. Next draw the roof lines of the mill. Draw the horizontal roof lines first and then the lines of the roof peak.

e. Continue to draw windows, doors, etc. until the mill is complete.

13. Draw the ground contour lines and rock formations.

14. Continue until all the lines of the tracing have been transposed to the full-size cartoon. See Illustration 1.3 on the next page.

15. Stand back from the drawing and look at the design's composition. Now is the time to make changes in the position of objects for composition or creativity.

16. Trace over all pencil lines with a black Sharpie® pen.

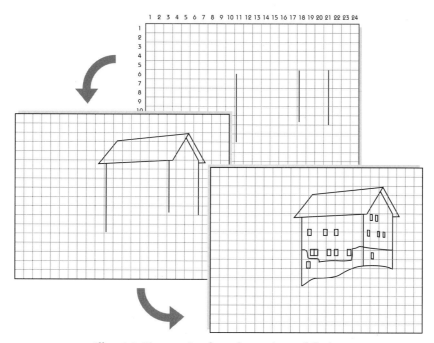

Illus. 1.2. Transposing from the tracing to full-size.

During this process, many of my students decide to plot out the points and then connect them with free-hand drawn lines. Remember to keep your hand and wrist loose to allow for freedom of movement. You do not need to make an exact copy; let your style emerge. When the initial full-size cartoon is complete, you can add, eliminate, or alter lines.

Illus. 1.3. Full-size cartoon.

LABELING THE CARTOON

Every object and area in the cartoon needs to be numbered. Start at the bottom and work your way to the top. Along the borders, mark each area that touches the border with the word END. Write notes on the cartoon concerning three-dimensionality, colors, or fabric choices. Glue small squares of selected fabrics to the cartoon for future reference.

MAKING THE TEMPLATES

If the design is simple, you may wish to cut the full-size cartoon to make the templates. If your design is complicated, with more than fifty pieces or with many houses and trees, you may not wish to cut up the full-size cartoon. In this instance, the next step is to trace and to label every numbered area onto template material, such as tracing paper or butcher's paper. Because you have traced the lines with a black Sharpie® pen, they will be visible through the butcher's paper. If not, you may want to tape the cartoon and the butcher's paper to a window or light table and continue to trace. I generally trace all individual components such as houses, trees, windows, doors and chimneys separately and then cut through the full-size cartoon for the major land areas such as fields, mountains and sky. Once I have used the templates, I tape them back together. This prevents them from being misplaced.

18

CHAPTER TWO

ELEMENTS
OF
DESIGN

It is the purpose of design to communicate to the viewer the quilt designer's response to and interpretation of a place. The quilt designer wants others to view this scene through her eyes. Therefore, what becomes most important is the manner in which the quilt designer organizes the elements of the scene and her use of line, space and texture to best convey her feelings.

The first consideration is the format or shape of the piece. Different shapes and sizes evoke different responses from the viewer. A small format conveys a feeling of intimacy with the surroundings; a large format emphasizes the immensity and loneliness of a scene. The size and format of the work are also determined by the scale in which the designer enjoys working and by the wall space allotted for the piece.

The most common format available to the landscape quilter is the rectangle – both vertical and horizontal. The landscape fits into the rectangular format and this format generally suits the available wall space. The horizontal rectangle is used to depict a broad expanse – water, shorelines, prairies, cornfields, a panoramic view of mountains and valleys. The landscape, in the horizontal format, conveys a sense of calmness and portrays a pastoral, serene mood. The vertical format focuses on a portion of the larger landscape such as a waterfall, tree, cliff, window, mill, or skyscraper. This format is an energetic, forceful and intimate view of the scene.

The vertical and horizontal rectangles are not the only options open to the quilt artist. There are infinite shapes from which to choose: the square, oval, circle, or irregular shapes. To achieve an irregular shape, omit the sky and let the landscape itself form the shape. Example #1: In a scene of a mountain goat perched on a rocky crag, the shape of the piece would conform to the shape of the rocky crag if the artist were to omit the background sky. Example #2: In a pastoral scene of open fields with mountains in the distance and a tree in the foreground, the shape of the quilt would follow the shape of the background mountains and of the tree if the artist were to omit the sky.

Once the quilt artist has decided on the format or shape of the piece, the second consideration is the composition or division of space. Space strengthens the illusion of three dimensions and of distance. The space that surrounds an object defines its shape, separates it from other objects, and establishes it as a point of interest.

When dividing the space into various sizes, artists apply the principle of the threes, i.e., always use an odd number of spaces or an odd number of divisions. Landscapes have three major divisions: background (sky), middle ground (mountain range), and foreground (fields). This is not an absolute, however. The scene may actually have unlimited space divisions of varying sizes and shapes.

Illustration 2.1 demonstrates the principle that unequal spaces are more interesting than spaces divided in half. In drawing a landscape scene, never divide the space into equal parts; always use spaces which are varied in size. In studying Illustration 2.1, note that the diagonal lines create more dynamic spaces than the horizontal and vertical lines. The diagonal lines indicate dimension and move the viewer's eye across the scene.

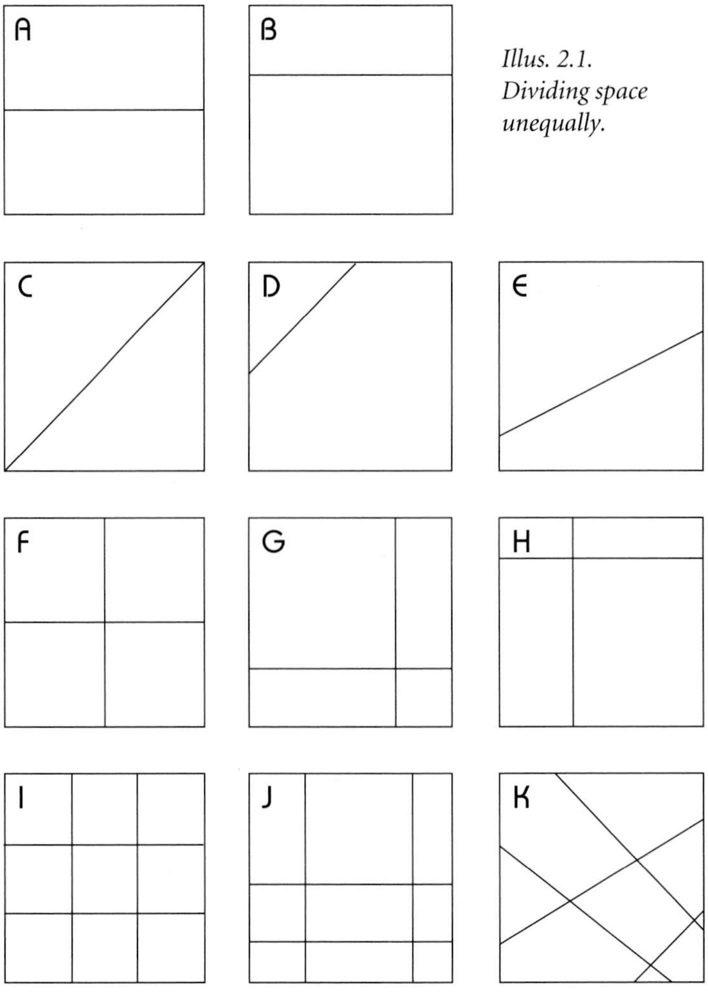

*Illus. 2.1.
Dividing space
unequally.*

Large spaces evoke a feeling of openness and freedom. The sky is the largest area of open space; it most often elicits a sense of serenity. To exaggerate the vastness of the sky, place the horizon line low and use the horizontal rectangle as the format. To create a scene that expresses vastness in the foreground such as beaches or deserts, place the horizon line high in the scene. Open areas in the design draw attention to and emphasize the focal point or the point of interest. When the scene is busy, the viewer's eye has no place to rest and the focal point will not be the predominant element. To create openness in a cluttered or busy landscape, add water, fog or snow to the scene. Illustration 2.2 is an example of creating openness in the landscape scene.

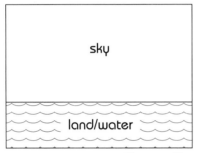 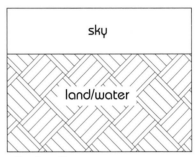

Illus. 2.2. Placement of horizon line.

All of the various space divisions within the quilt design are bounded by the edges of the quilt. The boundary frames the inner scene and keeps the viewer's eye from exiting the scene. Objects that have strong horizontal and vertical edges, such as trees and houses, should not be placed on the edge of the quilt. Illustrations 2.3-2.5 will help to explain.

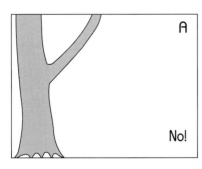

Do not place the base of a tree on the edge of the quilt. Move the base up from the edge an inch or so, or tilt the tree trunk inward so that the base extends into the border and is not seen. Illustration 2.3 explains.

Illus. 2.3. Placement of a tree.

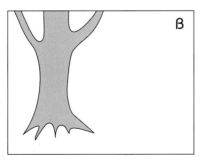 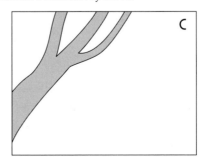

23

The same principal can be applied to a house. Do not place the house on the edges; move it into the quilt so that the entire house is visible or use the quilt border to conceal a portion of the house. Illustration 2.4 shows this concept.

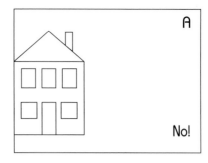

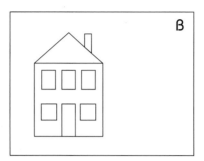

Illus. 2.4. Boundary.

When using trees to frame the scene, do not place the trees on the border; move them in from the border and place them off-center so that they divide the space in a more interesting manner. See Illustration 2.5.

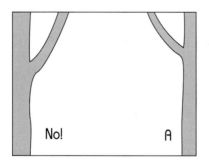
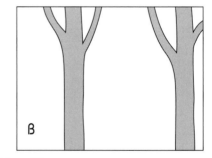

Illus. 2.5. Division of Space.

FOCAL POINTS

The quilt designer commands the viewer's attention by the placement of objects within the scene and by the variety of interesting spaces created. Each place where the eye rests is called a focal point or focal area and every landscape scene has one or more focal points and focal areas. Because the viewer's eye does not travel through the scene smoothly, but jumps from one focal point to the next, the placement of focal points is necessary to guide the viewer's eye through the scene and return it to the original focal point. The viewer's eye also follows lines within the quilt scene. Therefore, the quilt designer uses lines to direct the viewer's eye into the scene and not out. No lines should be drawn directly into a corner of the quilt because the eye would exit at that point. The illustrations on the next page help to explain.

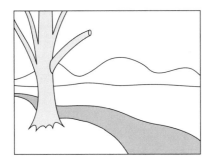

If a line such as a stream of water is leading out of the scene, block it with a tree so that the viewer's eye stops and bounces back into the center of the scene. See Illustration 2.6.

Illus. 2.6. Bring viewer's eye to center.

Do not begin a path in one corner of the quilt and continue it diagonally across the scene; move it in from the corner and then curve the path in toward the center of the scene. See Illustration 2.7.

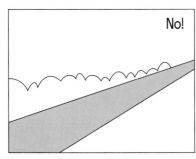
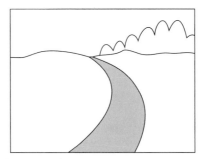

Illus. 2.7. Curve the path through the scene.

Avoid crowding objects of interest into a corner; place them closer to a focal area. If the focal area is located near the edge of the quilt, the viewer's eye exits the scene. If the focal area is located near the center of the quilt, the eye returns to the center. If the focal points are scattered over the quilt scene, the viewer's eye wanders aimlessly.

The placement of focal points within a scene permits the viewer's eye to travel through the scene and then to return to the original focal point or center of interest. The quilt artist may use any one of, or a combination of, the five basic follow-throughs shown here.

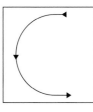

1. C

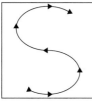

2. Inverted C

Illus. 2.8. Placement of focal point.

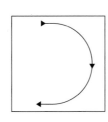

3. S

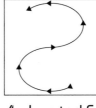

4. Inverted S

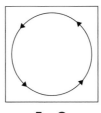

5. O

Illustration 2.9 shows that one method of positioning the focal points is to use the principle of the threes: divide the scene into thirds both horizontally and vertically so that there are four intersections of lines. By placing a design element on or near one of the four intersections, the element becomes a focal point. In order to create unity and balance, position a secondary object at the opposite diagonal intersection.

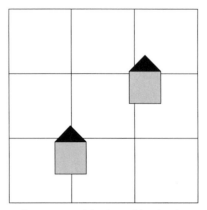

Illus. 2.9. Positioning of focal point.

Always keep the focal points well positioned. Do not place a focal point so near the border that it appears ready to exit the scene. Never place a person or an animal facing directly out of a scene or facing away from the focal point; always position the person and animal so that they are entering the scene and moving in the direction of the focal area.

When positioning trees near the border of the quilt scene, never lean the tree trunks out toward the borders. Always lean the tree trunks into the scene so that the viewer's eye moves up the tree trunk and along the branches into the center of the quilt. To create distance and space within a scene, the quilt designer may use a variety of lines that enables the viewer to enter the scene and to walk into the distance. The lead-in or entry line is used to lead the viewer's eye into the quilt and to guide the viewer to the focal area. Design elements may be placed along this line or at the intersections of the entry line with other ground contour lines. The best lead-in lines run diagonally across the quilt from near to far, from left to right, and then curve into the center of the scene. Fences, streams and winding dirt roads serve as interesting lead-in lines.

HORIZON LINE

The horizon line is the viewer's eye level as she views the scene. It should never be placed in the exact center of the scene; it should be positioned either above or below the center in order to create distance. By using a low horizon line, the background is enlarged; a great expanse of sky is created and the scene becomes more open. By using a high horizon line, the foreground is enlarged and a great expanse of ground or water appears. (Refer to Illustration 2.2 on page 23.)

Base lines and ground contour lines are also used to create distance in the quilt design. The base lines are those lines which run horizontally through a scene and depict variations in the ground contour. All vertical objects such as grasses, trees, shrubs and rocks emanate from the base lines. As base lines recede into the distance, the space between these lines becomes narrower. Place all trees, grasses, rocks and shrubs on different base lines to enhance the illusion of distance. The following examples demonstrate that as the ground recedes into the distance, the strips of ground become narrower.

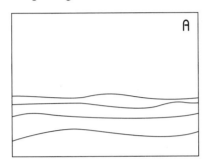

Draw the ground contour lines with wide spaces in the foreground; as the ground contour lines recede, the spaces between the lines become narrower. Review Illustration 2.10a and 2.10b.

Illus. 2.10. Ground Contour lines, above and with trees added at the right.

To make mountains appear larger, include one or two narrow strips of contour lines immediately in front of the mountains. See Illustration 2.11.

Illus. 2.11. Ground Contour lines and mountains.

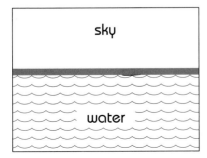

Use a dark, narrow strip to delineate the horizon line between water and sky, and to delineate the line between water and shore. See Illustration 2.12.

Illus. 2.12. Delineate between water and sky.

BANDING

Banding is a second technique employing ground contour lines. It uses the principle of the threes to create the illusion of depth in the scene. The foreground area is divided into three wide bands; the middle-ground is divided into two bands which are less wide; the background is drawn using one narrow band. See Illustration 2.13.

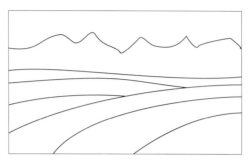

Illus. 2.13. Banding.

OVERLAPPING

Overlapping is the placement of one object behind another object to imply three dimensions and depth. The object which is in front appears to be closer to the viewer and the object which is behind appears to be further away from the viewer. By drawing several overlapping objects in diminishing sizes, the quilt designer enhances the illusion of depth. The following examples illustrate this technique.

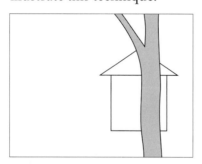

Illus. 2.14. Overlapping a tree.

Place a tree in front of a building or house so that it hides part of the building. See Illustration 2.14.

Place some objects below the horizon line, and place smaller objects on the horizon line. Position the smallest objects behind the horizon line. Illustration 2.15 depicts overlapping rocks in diminishing sizes.

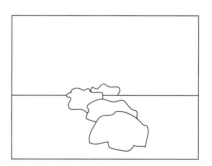

Illus. 2.15. Objects below horizon.

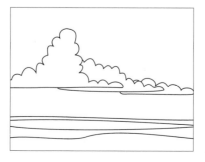

Draw overlapping clouds which diminish in size as they recede into the distance. Cloud streaks also diminish in width as they recede into the distance. Illustration 2.16.

Illus. 2.16. Overlapping clouds.

To emphasize the distance of an object that is in the background, place another object of known size in the foreground. This works best if the known object (person, tree, animal) is in the immediate foreground. Since the approximate size of the object in the foreground is known, it acts as a visual clue to indicate the sense of space that separates the two objects.

Without much knowledge of perspective the quilt artist can create a realistic scene. By overlapping or placing one object in front of another, the object which is behind is perceived to be further away. By placing one object higher up in the scene, it is perceived to be further away. By using a side view of an object rather than a front view, depth is emphasized.

Trees along a mountainside or on the slope of a hill become smaller as they approach the horizon line. We know that the trees are not smaller in size; they appear smaller in perspective. Illustration 2.17explains.

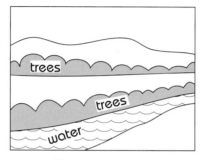

Illus. 2.17. Linear perspective.

Linear perspective is the use of lines and angles to create the illusion of dimension and depth. It is based on the use of the horizon line and the vanishing point. The horizon line is always at eye level. The vanishing point is a point along the horizon line or eye level line where all lines perpendicular to the horizon line seem to converge. The vanishing point may be inside or outside the actual landscape scene. See Illustration 2.18.

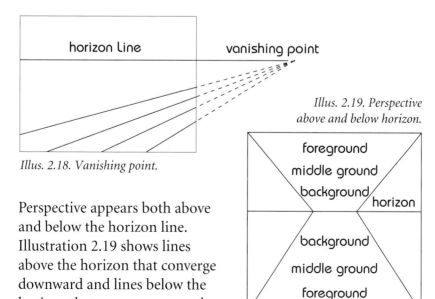

Illus. 2.18. Vanishing point.

Illus. 2.19. Perspective above and below horizon.

Perspective appears both above and below the horizon line. Illustration 2.19 shows lines above the horizon that converge downward and lines below the horizon that converge upward.

The quilt designer may include any of the following objects in linear perspective to create the illusion of distance in the landscape scene:

railroad tracks	a fence
a street	clouds
a row of houses	mountains, cliffs, rocks
a row of trees	skyscrapers
telephone poles	

To draw a row of trees or houses or a fence that recedes into the distance, it is necessary to use the rules of perspective. The spaces between the trees become progressively smaller until the trees seem to touch in the background. Following the steps in Illustration 2.20 below will help you understand how to divide depth into equal parts.

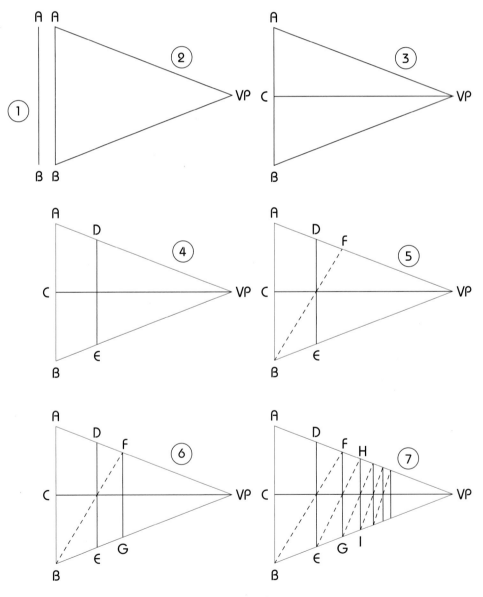

Illus. 2.20. Dividing depth into parts.

To draw a field with furrows, it is necessary to draw a horizon line and a vanishing point. Along the border of the design, make marks for the number of furrows you wish to include. From these marks, draw diagonal lines to the vanishing point. Illustration 2.21.

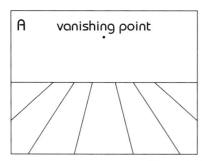 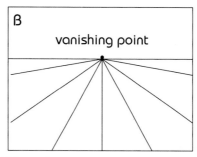

Illus. 2.21. Vanishing point.

Aerial perspective refers to the way the atmosphere alters the appearance of light. As distance increases, the atmosphere scatters more light causing the object to become increasingly lighter in value. The following rules apply:

1. All colors, except white, become cooler in temperature and lighter in value as they recede into the distance.

    a. White becomes slightly warmer and darker as it recedes.

    b. Yellow fades into gold and eventually disappears from the scene.

2. Objects in the distance take on a blue cast.

    a. As the yellows diminish, the violets and blues increase.

    b. Violets eventually give way to blues.

    c. Mountain ranges take on a pale purple or blue tinge as they recede into the distance.

3. Near objects tend to be brighter than distant objects.

4. Near objects have the greatest amount of detail. Only the broad shape of objects is discernible in the distance.

5. Near objects have the greatest amount of light/dark contrast.

    a. As trees recede into the distance, the light/dark contrast on the side of trees becomes less distinct.

    b. A path becomes lighter as it recedes.

    c. Shadows become progressively lighter as they recede into the distance.

Every tree has its own unique shape with bends, gnarls, knots
and root systems that differentiates it from any other. The best
way to do justice to the tree is to draw it in the field. If this is
not possible, refer to your photos and sketches of the tree or to
botanical books which contain drawings of the tree. As trees
recede into the distance, their base lines are closer together and
the tree trunks become narrower. As the tree becomes taller, the
trunk lines come closer together.

Most tree limbs tend to lift upward.
Limbs do not protrude from the trunk
in a symmetrical manner, i.e., one limb
does not grow out from the trunk
directly opposite another limb; rather
they grow out from the trunk at
staggered intervals. Illustration 2.22
depicts this. Place some limbs in front
of leaves and other limbs behind and
partially concealed by leaves. The limbs
and leaves that are behind are darker in
value than those limbs and leaves in

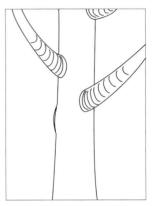

Illus. 2.22. Tree trunk.

the foreground. Vary the leaf clusters; create interesting shapes.
Allowing the sky to show through the leaves of the tree adds
dimension to the scene and permits the tree to breathe. Trees
that are located in the foreground must be more animated than
trees in the distance and they must contain details such as trunk
grooves, bark, severed limbs, roots and even blades of grass in the
shadow of the tree.

Rocks need angles, planes, edges and shadows to give them form,
dimension, and the sense of weight or volume. Rocks may be
angular and coarse or rounded and smooth. To make rocks
appear more rugged, place them near objects with contrasting
textures such as clouds, water, sand, earth and tree branches.
Rocks that are in the foreground need more detail such as cracks,
fractures, and crevices. As the rocks recede into the distance,
their size diminishes and there is less detail. In a scene that
contains many rocks, there will be groupings of rocks in which
some rocks will protrude, some will be jagged and rough, and
others will be smooth and rounded. With so many rocks
included in one scene, it is necessary to have an area of openness
in which the viewer's eyes may rest. In positioning the rock
groups, never allow the lines of one rock to lead directly to the
corner of another rock. These lines should run behind each other
so that the principle of overlapping becomes relative. Rocks need
shadows to give them solidity and volume. Decide the direction
of the light source. The planes of the rock that do not face the
light source will be in shadow and the rocks themselves will also

cast shadows on the ground. Use the baseline of the rocks to determine the position of the shadows. Remember that as baselines recede into the distance, they become increasingly pale. Refer to Illustration 2.23a, b, c, and follow these basic steps when drawing rocks:

1. Draw the general outline of the rock.

2. Divide this area into planes.

3. Decide the direction of the light source.

4. Separate the planes into values of light, medium and dark.

5. Add details such as crevices and fractures.

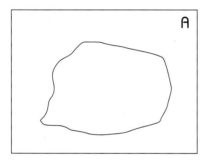

Illus. 2.23. Drawing rocks.

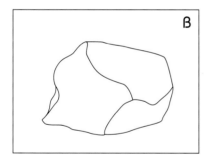

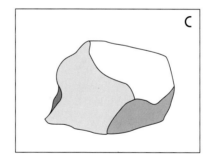

When drawing a mountain range or mountain ridge, do not repeat the ridge lines; vary the ridge peaks. Place a peak against a valley and a valley against a peak. Vary the size of the peaks and valleys as seen in Illustration 2.24. Once the peaks and valleys are drawn, draw the ridges that run down the mountainside.

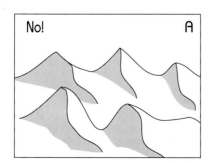

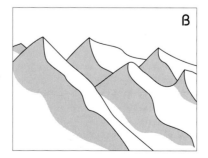

Illus. 2.24. Ridge peaks should be different sizes.

For the landscape artist, it is not essential to depict the correct cloud formation but rather to choose the cloud formation that is pleasing to the particular scene. If the amount of sky visible in the landscape scene is minimal, it is possible to have a cloudless sky. Even though there are no visible clouds, there will be a change of coloration in the sky due to the principle of aerial perspective. If the amount of sky visible is great, the sky must contain clouds, cloud streaks or, at the least, color variations In a daytime scene, no part of the sky will be completely dark.

In a landscape scene in which there is complexity in ground forms, keep the sky simple. If the ground forms are simple and flat, then a complex cloud formation is appropriate. When the ground forms are horizontal, arrange the cloud formations in a vertical manner.

Cloud streaks which disappear behind the hills and trees add depth to the scene. When drawing cumulus clouds, the upper portion of the clouds are arched with large billows and the bottoms of the clouds are nearly flat. In many instances, the bottoms of the cumulus clouds are hidden behind the hillsides. When drawing the cumulus cloud billows, keep the little puffs out of the large cloud billows. The little puffs should be draw at the corners of the large billows. See Illustration 2.25.

Illus. 2.25. Drawing cumulus clouds and cloud billows.

CHAPTER THREE

COLOR AND FABRIC CHOICES

Color choices are personal and intuitive. The colors the quilt designer chooses express her feelings about the scene; they create energy and imply distance in the scene and elicit an emotional response from the viewer. Some quilters have a natural sense or intuition for color; others have studied color theory and apply these rules to their quilts. If you do not have a formal knowledge of color theory, the best way to learn about color is to work with it. Other suggestions are as follows:

1. Study color theory in formal art classes.

2. Study the paintings of famous artists.

3. Take workshops on color with other quilters.

4. Study the quilts of famous quilters.

5. Experiment with structured color themes until you gain confidence and until your own color choices become more intuitive.

The artist uses color to evoke a mood or feeling; as symbols to express how she feels and to create distance within the scene. When studying the color combinations of famous paintings or quilts, ask yourself why you like or dislike the color combinations. How do you respond to the color combinations? Do the color choices evoke a sense of calm and serenity or do the color choices express energy and movement? Does the use of color create distance within the scene? Remember that there are no right or wrong color combinations in nature; nature contains all color combinations. If you were to look out over a field, you would see every possible shade of green juxtaposed against every other shade of green.

COLOR WHEEL

No matter how intuitively the quilter uses color, a basic understanding of the principles of color is indispensable. The color wheel, a device used by artists to understand color relationships, is made up of twelve pure colors that are equidistant from each other. Illustration 3.1 on the following page shows a simple color wheel. A pure color is one in which no black or white has been added. The three primary colors, red, yellow, and blue are pure colors – they exist by themselves and cannot be made by mixing two colors together. From these three primary colors, all other colors can be mixed. Of the three primary colors, pure yellow is the lightest color both in its value and its weight. Pure blue is the darkest in value and the heaviest in weight. When viewed emotionally or psychologically, yellow is the most animated; red is the most dynamic and energetic, and blue is the most reserved or calm of the three.

The secondary colors are formed by mixing two primary colors in equal proportions and are located on the color wheel exactly midway between the primary colors. The three secondary colors are orange, green, and violet. Orange is created from equal proportions of red and yellow; green from equal proportions of yellow and blue; violet from equal proportions of red and blue.

The tertiary colors are made by mixing equal proportions of one primary and one secondary color which are adjacent to each other on the color wheel. The six tertiary colors are red-orange, yellow-orange, yellow-green, blue-green, blue-violet and red-violet.

The complimentary colors are colors that are opposite each other on the color wheel and are also opposite each other in color temperature. The complimentary color is also the primary color which was not used in the mixing of the secondary color. For example, the primary colors blue and yellow are mixed to produce green. Red is the complement of green because it was not used in the mixing of green. The complementary colors are red and green, yellow and violet, blue and orange, blue-violet and yellow-orange, yellow-green and red-violet, and blue-green and red-orange.

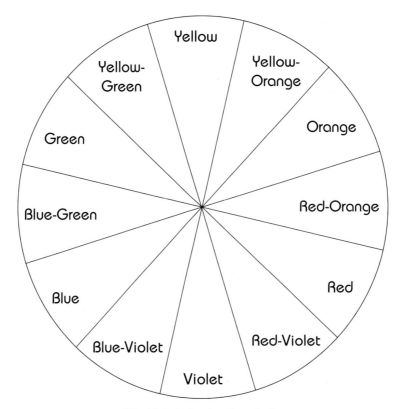

Illus. 3.1. A simple color wheel.

In working with color relationships and with fabric, the quilt artist needs to understand the three color terms: *hue, intensity,* and *value.*

Hue is the actual color of the fabric; it is another way of saying color. Intensity is color in its purest, brightest state. An intense or saturated color may be diluted by mixing it with black or white. To make a color appear more intense, place it next to its complimentary color. For example, by surrounding a pure green with its compliment red, the green will intensify or become stronger.

Value refers to the degree of lightness or darkness of a color. By adding black or white to a pure color, a range of light to dark values of that color can be created. By adding black to a hue, a darker value called a shade is produced. By adding white to a hue, a lighter value called a tint is produced. By adding grey to a hue, a tone or greyed version of the hue is produced.

Colors that are light in value reflect light and seem to advance. Colors that are dark in value tend to recede. The value of any color is relative to the color that surrounds it. Our perception of the color red changes as soon as it is surrounded with a second color. Black or any strong color which surrounds a red shape, will make the red shape seem lighter, brighter and larger than it really is. Because the red appears to come forward or advance, we perceive it to be closer than the black. When white surrounds the red shape, it makes the red shape seem darker, duller, and smaller than it really is. The red appears to recede and be further away than the white. The quilt artist can use these value changes to emphasize the illusion of depth and three dimension; to define the space around the object; to blend one area into another; or to separate the areas and objects of the scene.

In working with color relationships, an understanding of the concept of warm and cool colors is essential. Look at the color wheel again to determine which colors are considered to be warm and which colors are considered to be cool. The warm colors are yellow, yellow-orange, orange, red-orange, and red. The cool colors are violet, blue-violet, blue-green, and green. Red-violet and yellow-green are located on the line dividing the warm and cool colors. Therefore, they may be warm or cool depending on the color that surrounds them. If the surrounding color is cool, red-violet and yellow-green will appear warm; if the surrounding color is warm, red-violet and yellow-green will appear cool.

Warm colors advance and cool colors recede; warm colors tend to rise and cool colors tend to move downward; warm colors tend to be light in weight and cool colors tend to be heavy in weight. Color temperature can be used to evoke certain atmospheric conditions, to evoke moods or feelings such as loneliness, or to create the illusion of depth in the scene. To create a scene with fog, snow, mist or drizzle, use an analogous color scheme. An analogous color scheme uses adjacent colors on the color wheel such as blue-violet, blue, and blue-green. Use blue-violet, blue, and blue-green to create a wintry scene; use red, red-violet and violet to create a hot, dry, dusty scene. The illusion of depth can also be increased by using overlap and transparency. When two colors overlap each other, one appears to be behind the other. In the overlapping space a third or transparent color is produced. The transparent color is an intermediate value between the two original colors. Of the two original colors, the one which has the darker value appears to be further away and the lighter of the two original colors appears to be closer.

LIGHT AND SHADOW

In order to make the landscape scene more realistic and in order to add dimension and depth, it is essential to establish the light source and to indicate shadows. There are three sources of light: front light, side light and back light. When the source of light comes from behind the viewer and illuminates the scene in front of her, it is front light. Objects in the scene are detailed and little of the object is hidden by shadows. When the light source is either to the left or to the right of the viewer, it is called side light. The objects in the landscape are now seen in both light and shadow. An object in the light is more detailed than an object in a shadowed area. Because objects in the shadows are less detailed, only the general shapes and textures of the objects are apparent. Side light adds dimension to the scene, makes the forms emerge and lengthens the shadows. When the scene is between the viewer and the light source, it is called back light. Two excellent examples of backlighting are sunrise and sunset. All upright objects on the ground (trees, buildings, people) are viewed in strong silhouette with minimal details and the undersides of the clouds are bright.

In a moonlit scene, the moon must be the brightest white and the color white must be used sparingly elsewhere. The only objects that reflect bright light in a moonlit scene are windows and water. Because moonlight is backlighting, the ground objects are viewed in silhouette and the scene is monochromatic, i.e., one hue is visible in many values.

Shadows add reality, volume, weight, and depth to the landscape scene. They reveal the distance between objects and indicate to the viewer whether the objects are close together or far apart. A tree that is nearby casts a very dark shadow with clearly defined lines; a tree that is further away or even out of the scene, casts a softer, lighter shadow with very soft edges. Elongated shadows exaggerate the illusion of depth in the scene. Shadows which fall across another object (the shadows of tree branches on a tree trunk, for example) add dimension and volume to the objects and indicate the roundness of the object. Because clouds diffuse the light, they cast shadows on the ground and change the value of the land below.

Shadows indicate the direction of the light source and the time of day. When the light source is from the left, objects are cast in light on the left side and in shadow on the right side. In the late afternoon, the sun is low in the sky and the shadows that are cast are elongated and have a strong bluish purple color. Consider using these bluish purple shadows to add dark, cool colors to a warm scene.

The quilt artist uses the medium of fabric to express color and depth in the landscape scene. The design and texture of each fabric influences the manner in which color, dimension, time of day, season, mood and temperature of the scene are perceived by the viewer. Therefore, the fabric selection for the landscape quilt differs from the selection of fabric for a geometric quilt. The designer not only thinks in terms of hue and value but also in terms of scale and texture. She does not think in terms of mono-chromatic or analogous color schemes so much as in terms of fabric design and scale of the design. Does a particular fabric's design and scale of design depict a specific element of the land-scape scene? Does it reflect atmospheric conditions? Does it add the illusion of depth to the scene? Does this brown plaid depict tree bark? Does this green viney floral print depict grass? Does this stripe depict the wooden side of a barn?

The landscape designer no longer looks at a blue fabric solely for its color. She looks at the texture of the blue fabric to see if it represents water or sky. Does this marbled blue fabric represent a clear sky, a midnight sky, or a snowy sky? Does the design of the fabric lend itself to depicting movement in the sky? Does the fabric design suggest clouds or cloud streaks?

Because each fabric must contribute to the total effect of the scene, it is necessary to understand the terms *visual texture, scale* and *contrast.*

Visual texture, in this instance, refers to the way the fabric looks rather than to the way it feels. Another word for visual texture is design. In creating a landscape quilt, the designer needs fabric with a wide variety of visual textures, i.e., florals, paisleys, chintzes, geometrics, plaids and stripes. There are not many visual textures deemed inappropriate for landscape appliqué. The most difficult to use are fabrics such as diagonal stripes, plaids, large dots, circles or stars that have a high light/dark contrast.

Contrast refers to the difference between the light/dark values of the design motif. A fabric motif printed in two values of blue is a low contrast fabric; a fabric printed in white and navy blue is a high contrast fabric. For landscape appliqué, it is advisable to avoid fabrics with a strong light/dark contrast such as white and one other dark color or fabrics with equal amounts of two colors. They tend to be very busy and stand out from the other fabrics.

Scale refers to the size of the motif on the printed fabric; the quilt designer needs to use a variety of small, medium and large design motifs in order to create the illusion of depth in the scene. Large scale prints, such as paisleys, chintzes, florals and swirls, and bright, pure colors are used in the foreground to fill in large areas and to indicate detail and proximity to the viewer. The fabric's motif decreases in size and intensity as the distance from the viewer increases. To denote objects that are in the background of the scene, small scale motifs with low contrast are required. In this location, fabrics with high contrast are conspicuous.

PLAIDS AND STRIPES

The use of stripes within a landscape quilt suggests direction, distance, movement and different planes. Stripes lead the eye into the scene and then into the background. There are several types of stripes that may be used in a landscape quilt: the border print, the floral print stripe, the geometric print stripe and the stripe without a printed motif. Avoid using the wide border print stripe within the landscape scene itself and reserve its use for the borders. Narrow floral and geometric stripes (1"-1½" wide) make excellent inner borders which frame the landscape scene and are used to depict plowed fields and gardens. To use a floral or geometric stripe for fields or gardens, first draw a directional arrow on the field template to indicate the direction of the furrows; then align this arrow onto the stripe fabric so that the arrow and the stripe point in the same direction. It is not essential to use a stripe to depict fields and gardens. Consider floral motifs that are printed in diagonal rows and also fabrics in which the floral motifs are evenly spaced. The stripe which contains no motifs is best suited for depicting architectural details such as wooden beams, the wooden siding of a house, a log cabin, tin roofing, awnings, window sills, and door frames.

Shirting stripes and pastel plaids and stripes may be used to depict clouds, cloud streaks and the background sky. Using striped fabric adds diagonal movement to the sky. (See *Basque Fishing Village*.) Fabric which contains a woven metallic thread gives the appearance of rays of sunlight streaking through the sky. Use large floral chintz fabrics to depict cumulus clouds. Because even the bleakest expanse of sky contains color variations, many marbled or batiked fabrics are suitable. To audition a sky fabric, place the fabric behind the pieced foreground; move the fabric so that the marbled or batiked design runs diagonally behind the foreground. Continue to reposition the background fabric until it depicts the cloud movement appropriate for the scene.

Plaids with medium or low contrast are well suited to landscape design. Small symmetrical plaids may be employed to indicate brick, stone, tile roofs, and sidewalks. Larger plaids may be used to indicate stones, rocks, boulders, houses, fir trees, shadows, cloud streaks or sky.

Because landscape quilts are most often made for the wall rather than the bed, many fabrics such as voile, rayon, and dotted Swiss, which are unsuitable for the bed quilt, may be included within the landscape wall quilt. To make window panes appear transparent, cover the window pane fabric with a layer of light blue or light grey voile. In a contemporary landscape, the window pane fabric could be covered with a layer of clear vinyl. To portray falling snow and snowflakes, place a layer of dotted Swiss over the background sky. To depict the light which is reflected on the water, include fabrics such as moiré, taffeta or satin.

Windowscape #1: Morning
27" x 37"
1986, Sheryl Morrow Robinson

Hand pieced; Hand appliquéd;
Hand quilted; Beading.

Windowscape #2: Midday
29" x 39"
1986, Sheryl Morrow Robinson

Hand and machine pieced;
Hand quilted; Beading;
Three-dimensional stuffed leaves.

Windowscape #3: Midnight
28" x 38"
1986, Sheryl Morrow Robinson

Hand appliqué; Machine pieced borders; Hand quilted; Beading; Three-dimensional stuffed birds.
(In the collection of W. L. Mariott.)

Windowscape #4: Twilight
28" x 39"
1986, Sheryl Morrow Robinson

Hand appliquéd; Machine pieced;
Hand quilted; Painting;
Three-dimensional reeds.

Taxco
37" x 37"
1984, Sheryl Morrow Robinson

Hand appliquéd;
Hand quilted; Painted; Beaded;
Metallic embroidery;
Three-dimensional leaves.

(above) Landscape: The Snowfall
51" x 45"
1988, Sheryl Morrow Robinson

Hand pieced; Hand quilted.
From a painting by
Canadian artist, A. J. Casson.

Windowscape #5: The Storm
28" x 38"
1986, Sheryl Morrow Robinson

Hand appliqué; Machine pieced
borders; Hand quilted; Beading;
Three-dimensional stuffed trees.

Kristofer's Neighborhood
60" x 80"
1985, B. J. Elvgren

Hand appliqué; Hand quilted; Hand painted.

Sheepfold
46" x 47"

1984, B. J. Elvgren
Hand appliqué; Hand
quilted; Hand painted.

Viva Haiti!
64" x 63"
1984, B. J. Elvgren

Hand appliqué; Hand
quilted; Hand painted.

Landscape: The Sheep
43" x 34"
1987, Sheryl Morrow Robinson

Hand appliqué; Machine pieced
borders; Painting; Prairie Points.

Autumn Forest
41" x 48"
1990, D. Michaeline Reed

Machine appliqué; Machine
quilted; Fused.
Inspired by a photograph
by Bob Clemenz.

50

Escurra, Spain
43" x 39"
1985, Sheryl Morrow Robinson

Hand pieced; Hand appliqué;
Painted; Hand quilted.
Inspired by a National
Geographic photograph.

*Basque Fishing
Village*
49" x 48"
1985, Sheryl Morrow
Robinson

Hand pieced; Hand
quilted. Inspired from a
photo in one of my
Spanish books.

(In the collection of
Jemele Sanderson.)

Landscape: The Rabbits
50" x 43"
1988, Sheryl Morrow
Robinson

Hand appliqué; Machine
pieced borders; Hand quilted.
(In the collection of
Mary E. Duquin.)

*The Dance of
the Rabbits*
64" x 59"
1989, Sheryl
Morrow
Robinson

Machine pieced;
Hand appliqué;
Hand quilted.

Cream Tea in a Dorset Garden
60" x 80"
1989, B. J. Elvgren

Machine appliqué; Machine quilted; Hand painted.

Winter Landscape
58" x 48"
1989, Lisa Coate Sauer

Machine pieced; Hand appliqué; Reverse appliqué; Painted.
Inspired by a color etching from Susan Hunt Wulkowicz, entitled *Winter Fields*.

The Garden
40" x 50"
1988, Sheryl Morrow Robinson

Procion-dyed fabrics; Fabric painting; Hand appliqué; Hand quilted.
(In the collection of Mr. and Mrs. Ronald Schneider.)

Depth Charge #2:
The Sea Dragons
61" x 46"
1989-1990, Sheryl
Morrow Robinson

Machine pieced; Reverse
appliqué; Hand appliqué;
Painting; Beading;
Three-dimensional legs;
Couching.

Taking A Closer Look
40" x 42"
1990, B. J. Elvgren

Machine appliqué;
Machine quilted;
Hand quilted.

Depth Charge #1: A View Within
38" x 65"
1989, Sheryl Morrow Robinson

Machine pieced; Machine appliqué; Painting; Beading.

Free Range Eggs
42" x 48"
1990, B. J. Elvgren

Machine appliqué; Machine quilted; Hand pieced.

CHAPTER FOUR

APPLIQUÉ TECHNIQUES

Before marking fabric for either machine or hand sewing, press all fabrics to remove wrinkles and creases. To mark fabrics for hand appliqué, trace the templates onto the right side of the fabric. To mark templates for machine sewing, trace the templates onto the wrong side of the fabric. Use a mechanical pencil to mark the design onto light colored fabrics and use a white, yellow, or silver quilt marking pencil to mark the design onto dark fabrics.

When marking curved and circular templates, position the template on the bias rather than on the straight of grain of the fabric. This permits the fabric to roll under more easily as it is sewn. Mark all flower stems and tree branches on the bias of the fabric. The bias of the fabric permits the stems and branches to bend and curve at will.

1. Place the template onto the fabric so that the wrong side of the template is against the right side of the fabric.

2. Position the template onto the fabric to take advantage of the design motif. For example, when using a floral stripe to depict the rows of a flower garden, place the grainline arrow of the template onto the fabric so that the arrow and the stripe of the fabric run in the same direction (See Illustration 4.1.) Pin the template into position.

3. Using a mechanical pencil or a sharpened quilt marking pencil, trace around the outside of the template. Keep the point of the pencil close to the edge of the template to ensure accurate templates.

4. Cut out the fabric ¼" outside of the pencil line. (NOTE: When cutting out any template labeled END, leave a 1"-1½" seam allowance to allow for sewing variances.)

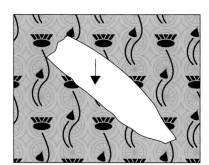

Illus. 4.1. Template positioned on the fabric with the grain line.

To make templates for freezer paper appliqué:

1. Trace every shape onto the shiny side of the freezer paper using a permanent marking pen such as a Sharpie®. (NOTE: If you wish to trace onto the dull side of the freezer paper, you must reverse all shapes that are asymmetrical.) The shapes may be traced close together because no seam allowance is added to them.

2. Cut out the freezer paper shapes carefully; the shape which is cut determines the final shape of the appliqué.

3. Iron the freezer paper shapes onto the wrong side of the fabric leaving ½" spaces between the shapes.

4. Cut out the fabric leaving a ¼" seam allowance beyond the freezer paper. (NOTE: When cutting out any template labeled END, leave a 1"-1½" seam allowance to allow for sewing variances.)

To mark templates for machine sewing:

1. Place the right side of the template onto the wrong side of the fabric. Pin the template into position leaving a ½" space between templates.

2. Trace around the outside of the template with a mechanical or quilt marking pencil.

3. Cut out ¼" beyond the pencil line. (NOTE: when marking any template labeled END, leave a 1"-1½" seam allowance to allow for variances in sewing.)

If the templates for machine sewing have straight edges, it is possible to omit the tracing step:

1 Pin the template into position and place the fabric onto a cutting mat.

2. Using a clear plexiglass ruler, place the ruler so that it extends ¼" beyond the template.

3. Roll the blade of the cutter along the edge of the ruler to cut the ¼" seam allowance.

4. Turn the fabric to continue this process until all straight edges of the template have been cut.

Once the fabrics have been prepared for appliqué, it is necessary to decide the order in which the pieces are to be sewn. I generally begin in the foreground and appliqué or piece from the front to the back. Follow these steps and refer to Illustration 4.2:

1. The closest strip of foreground is positioned on top of the strip of ground beyond it. Match the seam allowances of both pieces by sticking a pin through the foreground seam line into the seam line of the second piece.

2. Turn under the seam allowance of the front strip and position it on top of the back strip, hiding the two pencil lines.

3. Pin into position. Place the pins perpendicular to the folded edge to prevent the thread from becoming caught on the pins.

In sewing from the foreground to the background, it is often necessary to insert houses, trees and other objects that overlap the background. Turn under the ¼" seam allowance on the edges of the shapes which are to be inserted into the seam allowance. Insert the shape into the background and pin into position. (NOTE: It is possible to sew the background together without inserting houses or trees. Once the background has been sewn together, open up the seams, insert the houses and trees, pin into position and sew.)

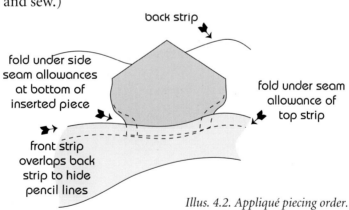

back strip

fold under side seam allowances at bottom of inserted piece

fold under seam allowance of top strip

front strip overlaps back strip to hide pencil lines

Illus. 4.2. Appliqué piecing order.

In needle turn appliqué, there is no pressing or basting under of the seam allowances. This is a time saving technique in which the quilter folds or rolls under the seam allowance with her needle as she sews to produce smooth, sharp edges. Follow these steps and refer to Illustration 4.3 for efficient needle turn appliqué:

1. Thread a number 11 Sharp needle with an 18" long single strand of thread that matches the color of the piece being appliquéd. Knot the thread.

2. Position the fabric shape to be appliquéd onto the background fabric. Pin into place.

3. Hold the fabric in your hands so that the seam allowances point away from you.

4. Begin to turn under the fabric in the least curved place. Turn under the seam allowance with your needle. Use the needle tip to smooth out any points.

5. Once you have turned under an inch or so, place your thumb atop the folded seam to hold it in position.

6. Insert the needle from the wrong side of the background fabric. Bring the needle up through the fold of the appliqué shape. Pull the needle and thread tight.

7. Insert the needle into the fabric directly below the place where it came up and also below the fold of the fabric.

8. Slide the needle to the left a scant ⅛" and bring the needle up through the fold of the fabric again. Pull thread tight.

9. Continue to sew in this manner spacing the stitches ¹⁄₁₆"-⅛" apart. Because the appliqué stitch produced is perpendicular to the fold rather than on a diagonal across the fold, less of the thread is visible on top of the fabric.

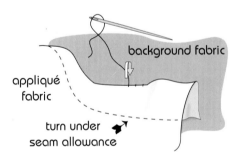

Illus. 4.3. Needle turn applique stitch.

It is important to keep the stitching as unobtrusive as possible. To do this, use a thread that matches the appliqué shape; use an appropriate stitch, such as the tack stitch described above or the blind stitch; keep the tension uniform by giving a light tug on the thread; and space the stitches no further than ⅛" apart.

To make sharp points on leaves refer to Illustration 4.4 a, b, c:

1. Sew up to the point with tiny tack stitches.

2. Fold under the seam allowance to the left.

3. Take another stitch in the point to anchor it and to keep it intact.

4. Once the point has been secured, cut out excess fabric in the right hand seam allowance.

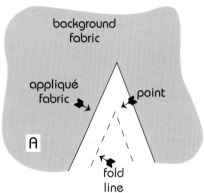

Illus. 4.4a. Achieving sharp points.

5. Fold under the left hand seam allowance and continue to sew.

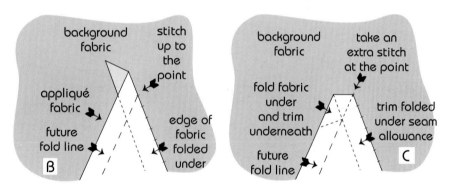

Illus. 4.4b and 4.4c. Follow these illustrations to achieve sharp points.

To sew an inverted point or corner, follow these steps and refer to Illustration 4.5a, b and c on the following page:

1. Sew as close to the point as possible before cutting. When it is no longer possible to turn under the seam allowance easily, clip through the seam allowance to within one or two threads of the pencil line.

2. Turn under the seam allowances on both sides of the inverted point. To prevent further unraveling of threads, use the side of the needle or a moistened toothpick to turn under any stray threads.

3. Place your thumb on the corner to hold it in position as you sew toward it.

4. Sew directly to the point, making stitches closer together as you near the point.

5. Bring up the needle 2-3 threads from the point. Insert the needle into the background fabric and give a tug on the thread to pull under any stray threads.

6. Make another tack stitch on top of the previous one in the corner. Continue to sew.

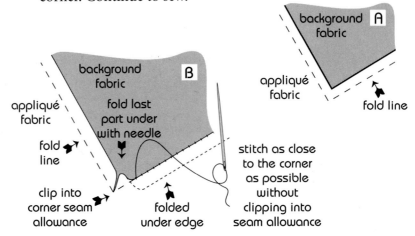

Illus 4.5a and 4.5b demonstrate inverted points and corners.

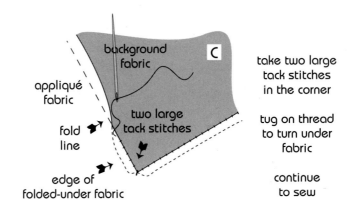

Illus. 4.5c. Tack stitch the corner to control stray threads.

REVERSE APPLIQUÉ

Appliqué is the technique in which one or more pieces of fabric are applied or sewn on top of a background fabric. As successive layers are added, the surface design is built up on the background fabric. In reverse appliqué, the background fabric is cut to expose the layers of fabric beneath it. As successive layers are cut and sewn, the design is built down from the background to imply depth. To reverse appliqué, follow these steps and refer to Illustration 4.6a, 4.6b, 4.6c:

1. Lightly trace the design onto the background fabric.

2. Pin or baste at least ¼" outside the pencil line. Baste only for large projects.

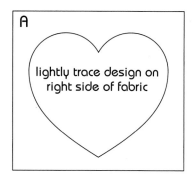
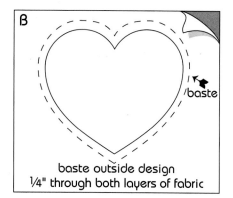

Illus 4.6a and 4.6b. Reverse appliqué.

3. With the tips of sharp embroidery scissors, pierce the background fabric within the pencil lines. Trim away the excess fabric to within ³⁄₁₆" of the pencil line. Be careful not to snip the fabric to be exposed.

4. Clip into curves and corners when necessary, stopping within one thread of the pencil line.

5. Fold under the fabric on the pencil line and finger press. Hold the fold in place with your thumb as you sew.

6. Turn fabric to the wrong side and trim excess fabric to within ¼" of the sewn line.

7. If you wish to expose a third layer of fabric, baste a fabric square of contrasting color beneath the second layer. This square

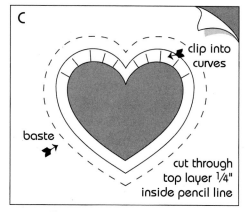

Illus. 4.6c. Depicts steps 6 and 7.

must be at least one inch larger than the shape to be exposed. Trace the new shape within the first shape. Continue with step 3.

The reverse appliqué technique may be used to imply depth and dimension in such objects as flowers, doors, and windows. To achieve this, follow these steps and refer to Illustration 4.7a, b, c:

1. Trace the outline of the house, windows and doors onto the house fabric. Mark lightly with a mechanical pencil and ruler.

2. Cut a piece of door fabric at least one inch larger than the finished door. If there is a row of three or four windows across the front of the house, cut a strip of fabric that is one inch longer and wider than the row of windows. If there is only one window, cut the window fabric one inch larger than the finished window.

3. Pin the right side of the door and window fabrics to the wrong side of the house fabric. Stick a pin through the pencil line to the wrong side of the fabric. Turn the fabric to the wrong side and check to see that the window and door fabrics extend beyond all pencil lines. Reposition the window and door fabrics if necessary. Once again, basting is optional. It is also possible to pin on the wrong side of the fabric, so that the thread does not catch onto the pins as you sew.

4. Pierce the house fabric with embroidery scissors and trim away the excess fabric. Leave a ³⁄₁₆" seam allowance. Snip into the nearest corner of the window and/or door. Do not cut all four corners at this time.

5. Fold under the seam allowance; finger press; hold in position with your thumb and sew. When you approach a corner, follow the guidelines given for inverted points.

6. When the sewing is completed, turn the fabric to the wrong side and trim the seam allowances to a quarter inch.

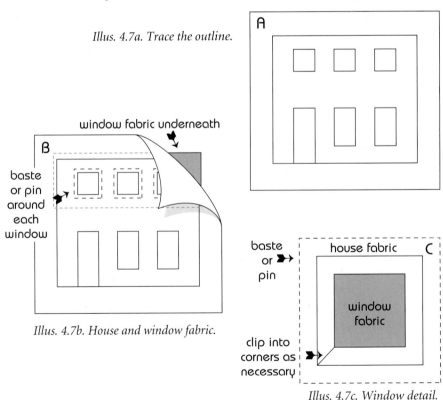

Illus. 4.7a. Trace the outline.

A

window fabric underneath

β

baste or pin around each window

Illus. 4.7b. House and window fabric.

baste or pin

house fabric   C

window fabric

clip into corners as necessary

Illus. 4.7c. Window detail.

Broderie perse is the term for needlework in which flower, bird and tree motifs were cut from chintz fabric, arranged into a pleasing design, and then appliquéd to the background fabric. Most often this style of appliqué was used in the central panel and borders of a tree of life medallion quilt (late 1700's to early 1800's) or in the blocks of friendship and album quilts of the 1840-1860 period. The chintz cutouts were appliquéd to the background fabric with the buttonhole stitch or the blind stitch. The broderie perse technique may be used today to embellish a landscape scene by using the chintz motifs as the flowers in a garden (*The Garden and Windowscape #1: Morning*) or as border elements.

To appliqué the chintz cutout with a blind stitch, follow the steps below and refer to Illustration 4.8 below:

1. Using small, well-sharpened embroidery scissors, cut out the chintz motif leaving a $\frac{3}{16}$" seam allowance.

2. Position the motif onto the background fabric. Pin or baste into position.

3. Using thread that matches the chintz, appliqué the chintz to the background fabric with the needle turn technique. Sew with small blind stitches or tack stitches.

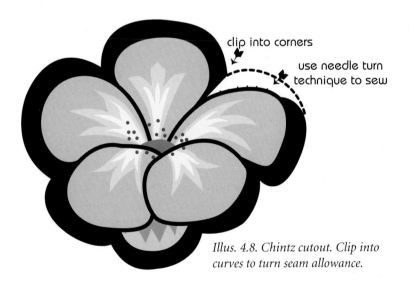

clip into corners

use needle turn technique to sew

Illus. 4.8. Chintz cutout. Clip into curves to turn seam allowance.

To appliqué the chintz cutout with the buttonhole stitch, follow these steps and refer to Illustration 4.9:

1. Cut out the chintz motif on its outline. No seam allowance is needed.

2. Position the motif onto the background fabric. Pin or baste into position.

3. Using thread that either matches or contrasts with the chintz, attach the chintz motif to the background fabric using a buttonhole, blanket or satin stitch.

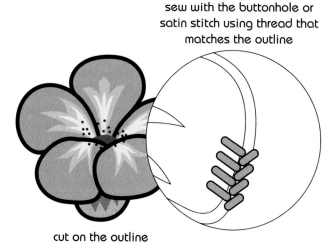

sew with the buttonhole or satin stitch using thread that matches the outline

cut on the outline

Illus. 4.9. Chintz cutout. Buttonhole stitch shown. Use matching thread.

THREE-DIMENSIONAL FLOWERS AND LEAVES

Three-dimensional flowers and leaves may be added to the landscape scene to portray depth and add interest to the foreground. Leaves made of a single layer of fabric are used as fill-in and as background; leaves of two or three layers are used as foreground and protrude from the quilt.

To make the three-dimensional leaves with and without batting:

1. Draw the leaf in at least three sizes on template plastic. Cut out the leaf templates.

2. Trace around the leaf with a mechanical pencil on the wrong side of the fabric. Be sure to leave a ½" space between leaves. Trace as many leaves as desired. I try to adhere to the rule of threes and draw an odd number in each of the three sizes. It is better to make too many leaves now, rather than to have to make more leaves later.

3. Place the right side of this fabric to the right side of a second green fabric which either matches or contrasts with the original green fabric. Pin the two layers together.

4. In order to make three-dimensional leaves with batting, add a layer of batting below the second green fabric. Pin all three layers together.

5. Machine or hand stitch on the pencil line in either of the following two methods:

   a. Sew on the line leaving a one inch opening. Trim the seam allowance to ⅜". Clip into the curves. Turn the leaf to the outside. Press. Close the opening with whipstitches.

   b. Sew completely around the leaf leaving no opening. Trim the seam allowance to ⅜". Clip into the curves. Using sharp embroidery scissors, pierce the back fabric and cut a slit 1"-1½" long. Be careful to keep this slit on the lengthwise or crosswise grain of the fabric. Turn the leaf inside out. Press. Close the opening with whipstitches.

   6. Pin leaves into position onto the background fabric.

   7. Because the leaves are three-dimensional and are to stand out from the background, appliqué only ⅓ of the way around the leaf. Leave the remainder of the leaf

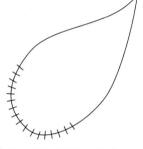

Illus. 4.10. Stitch only lower third of leaf.

FLOWERS

To make three-dimensional flowers, the basic techniques of constructing three-dimensional leaves are followed. Draw the flower petals in three sizes. Construct an odd number of single layer petals which are to be appliquéd to the background fabric. Construct an odd number of petals using two layers of fabric and an odd number of petals made of two layers of fabric plus one layer of batting.

To make stuffed flowers, follow these steps and refer to Illustration 4.11:

   1. Draw a full-size flower on paper. Cut out the templates.

   2. Pin the paper templates onto the right side of the fabric and trace around the templates. Cut out 4 or 5 petals from a single layer of fabric. Leave at least a ⅜" seam allowance.

   3. Pin the flower petals into position on the background fabric. As you pin the petals into position, push the fabric together so that a slight bulge in the fabric appears. Stitch around the petal leaving the center ends open. Stuff small amounts of polyester fiber into the petals.

4. Draw a flower center (circle) that is slightly larger than the center opening where the petals meet. Cut out the flower center with a ¼" seam allowance.

5. Pin into position, making certain that all raw edges of the petals are covered by the flower center.

6. Sew about ¾ of the way around the circle. Gently stuff with

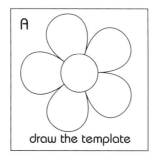

draw the template

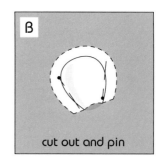

cut out and pin

Illus. 4.11. Making stuffed flowers.

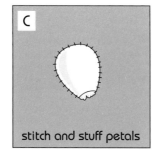

stitch and stuff petals

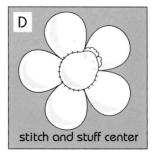

stitch and stuff center

RAW-EDGED FLOWERS

Some flowers such as geraniums and hydrangeas would be too time consuming to make with two layers of fabric. For this type of flower, make petals of only one layer. Follow these steps and refer to Illustration 4.12:

1. Draw the flower petal in three sizes. Make templates.

2. Trace the petals onto eight to ten solid color fabrics of different values. Each hydrangea or geranium requires 50 to 100 petals!

3. Cut out the petals on the traced line and place onto waxed paper.

4. In a well-ventilated room, apply Fraycheck™ to the raw edges of the petals and let dry. The Fraycheck™ may slightly darken the edges of the petals.

5. Sew the petals to the background. Attach only the center of the petals so that the edges remain free.

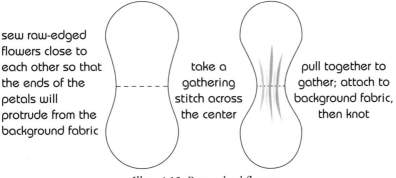

sew raw-edged flowers close to each other so that the ends of the petals will protrude from the background fabric

take a gathering stitch across the center

pull together to gather; attach to background fabric, then knot

Illus. 4.12. Raw-edged flowers.

One of the oldest techniques in quilting to make three-dimensional flowers is ruching, a technique in which folded strips of bias fabric were sewn in a zigzagged line and then gathered together to form chrysanthemums, zinnias, and roses. Ruching is found on appliqué album quilts of the second half of the 19th century, especially in the flower basket blocks of the Baltimore album quilts. Not only was it used for flowers but it was also used for stems and baskets staves. To make a ruched flower:

1. Cut a strip of fabric across the 45 inch width of the fabric. The width of the strip may vary from 1¼"-2" wide. Use a variety of widths to create flowers with different petal dimensions.

2. Fold in the raw edges along both sides of the strip wrong sides together until they meet in the center. Press with an iron.

3. Knot a long strand of thread (18"-20") that matches the fabric.

4. With small running stitches (8-10 per side), stitch in a zigzag or right angle line according to Illustration 4.13.

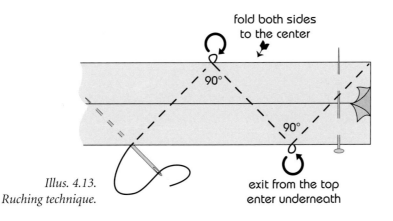

fold both sides to the center

90°

90°

Illus. 4.13. Ruching technique.

exit from the top enter underneath

5. It is necessary to loop the thread over the folded edge of the fabric so that the thread will not lock itself. As you reach the folded edge and the needle is on the side facing you, loop it to the back and insert it from the back to the front making sure that you do not catch the previous stitch.

6. Continue to sew for 8-10 inches, then gently gather the stitches to form the petal shapes as shown in Illustration 4.14. Knot the thread. If the thread were to break, all previously gathered petals would not unravel.

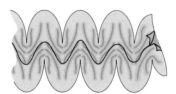

gently gather the stitches

Illus. 4.14. Gather stitches to form petals.

7. If the gathered petals are of varying sizes, the stitches were not sewn in uniform right angles. Mary Toda has suggested a technique to sew perfect right angles: Grasp the fabric strip in both hands. Use your right hand to fold down the strip so that the folded edge is vertical to the rest of the strip. Finger press the diagonal line, open up and sew along this crease. Make the thread loop. Now, with the left hand, fold down the fabric strip so that the folded edge is vertical to the rest of the strip. Finger press and sew. Refer to Illustration 4.15.

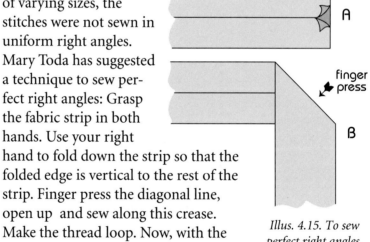

Illus. 4.15. To sew perfect right angles.

8. After ruching a distance of 12"-15", place the ruching on the background fabric to determine how much more is needed. Repeat steps 4-7 if needed.

9. To attach the ruched strip to the background fabric, begin on the outer rim of the circle and work in toward the center. Turn under the raw edge of the ruched strip ¼". Pin the strip into position so that all raw edges face the background fabric. Continue to pin the ruched strip until the outer circle is complete. With matching thread, attach the ruched strip to the background fabric by sewing down the center of the strip. For the second circle, the petals of the

ruched strip will overlap the gathering line of the first circle. Pin the second circle. Sew. Continue to the center of he circle. Turn under the raw edge of the ruched strip and tack into place. Illustration 4.16a and b show how this is done. A finished ruched circle is shown on the next page.

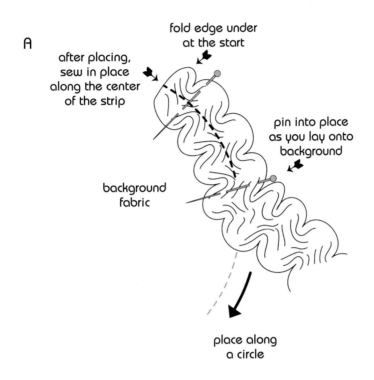

A

fold edge under
at the start

after placing,
sew in place
along the center
of the strip

pin into place
as you lay onto
background

background
fabric

place along
a circle

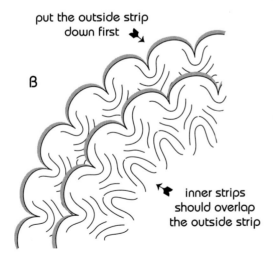

B

put the outside strip
down first

inner strips
should overlap
the outside strip

Illus. 4.16. Placing ruched strips around in a circle.

10. To make a ruched flower of two or more colors, gather a strip long enough for the outer circle. Then begin with a second color and follow the same procedure. Make two or more concentric rings of the second color. Complete the center of the flower with a third color.

Illus. 4.17. Completed ruched flower.

CHAPTER FIVE

EMBELLISHMENTS

When the words embellishment of quilts came to mind, I used to think of the embroidered and painted crazy quilts of the Victorian era. When I first began to quilt, to me, embellishment meant to make French knots for eyes and to use the running stitch for leaf veins. Today, embellishment means not only to embroider, but also to apply paints, beads, found objects, and metallic threads. To embellish means to improve the appearance of, to adorn, to make beautiful or elegant by ornaments. Every thread, ornament and drop of paint placed on the quilt surface is intended to add to and enhance the beauty of the surface design. The embellishment adds textural interest and integrates the patchwork and the found objects, paints and embroidery into a whole. Embroidery is often used to enhance the texture of the fabric, to complete an image with detail and to highlight an object or area. One of the easiest embroidery techniques to master which adds texture and dimension to a scene is couching.

COUCHING

Couching (shown in Illustration 5.1) is the laying on the surface of a cord or thick thread which is then secured into place with tiny stitches. It is an advisable technique to use for any thread which can not be threaded through the eye of a needle. One use of couching is to add lines of accent such as the veins of a leaf:

1. Choose a nubby thread to be laid down in the vein pattern.

2. For a couching thread select embroidery thread, pearl cotton, or metallic thread which matches the nubby thread.

3. Pin the nubby thread into position or hold it in position with your left hand.

4. Bring the couching thread up through the background fabric next to the nubby thread, cross over the nubby thread and enter the fabric on the opposite side of the nubby thread.

5. Continue to sew in this manner until the vein design is complete.

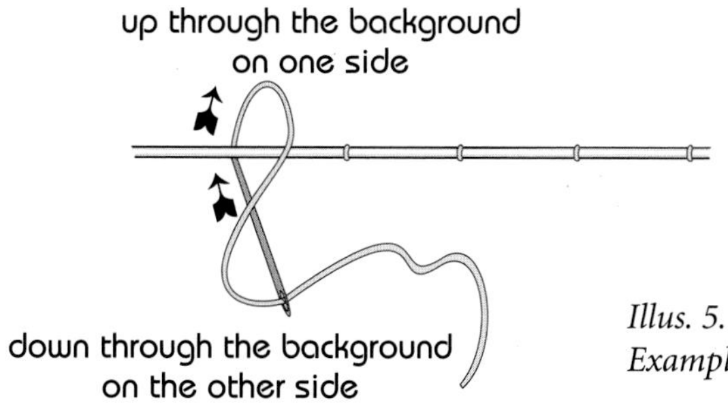

up through the background
on one side

down through the background
on the other side

Illus. 5.1.
Example of couching technique.

A second use of the couching technique is to outline reverse appliqué. The line of couched thread is placed along the inner edge of the reverse appliqué. The thread adds a contrasting color between the two layers of fabric and emphasizes the shape of the reverse appliqué. (See *Depth Charge #2: The Sea Dragons*.) It is also possible to couch strings, cords or knotted threads to portray grasses growing in a meadow.

EMBROIDERY STITCHES

Embroidery stitches (Illustration 5.2a, b, c) such as the stem, the running and the feather stitch may be used to outline areas. Satin stitches of irregular lengths are used to fill in an outlined area, to show grainline and tree bark, and to blend colors into one another. Beads and French knots may also be used to fill in outlined areas.

Embroidery done in wool is known as crewel work. Crewel is used to embellish flowers or animals and to show grainline or bark on a tree trunk. Work crewel with a large-eyed, blunt needle. When using any embroidery thread to accent areas in the landscape scene, change the color of the thread to reflect the visible amount of sunlight, i.e., embroider shadows in cool colors and sun filled areas in warm colors.

Many quilters think of the tying of threads as a technique to hold together the layers of a utilitarian quilt; it is also a technique to embellish the quilt. Use tying as a quilting technique for large areas on the landscape such as the sky, an expanse of water or large fields. The tied threads not only quilt the space but also add dimension and softness. A second use of tying is to give plants and grasses dimension:

1. Use six strands of embroidery thread cut into 18" lengths.

2. Take a stitch in the plant or grass, leaving a 2" strand.

3. Take a second stitch in the same place and tie together with two or three knots. Vary the length of the strands to produce uneven grass lengths.

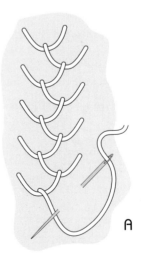

Illus. 52a. Feather stitch.

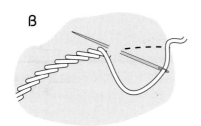

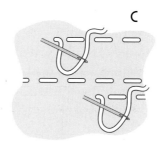

Illus. 5.2b. Outline or stem stitch.   *Illus. 5.2c. Running or darning stitch.*

Trapunto (Illustration 5.3) is high relief worked through two layers of cloth. The layers are tacked together and a thread is woven through the channels to form a three-dimensional design. Trapunto may be used to make ridges or furrows in a field or to delineate the boundaries between fields:

1. Place a layer of fabric, such as muslin, behind the field. Baste into place, then lightly sketch the design of the furrows onto the muslin.

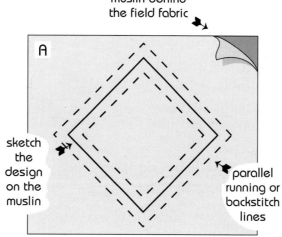

Illus. 5.3a. Trapunto.

2. Match the thread to the quilt top. On the muslin side of the fabric, sew parallel lines with small running stitches or the backstitch. These lines are sewn through both layers of the fabric and are spaced wide enough apart so that the cord may pass through the channels between them.

3. Run the cord through the channel with a blunt-tipped, large-eyed needle called a bodkin. For the cord, use wool or a highly twisted cotton such as mason's line.

4. Leave a loop of cord every 2"-3" so that it can be pulled to make the ridges and furrows.

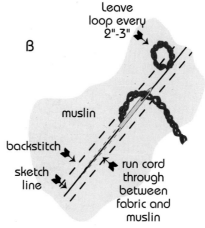

Illus. 5.3b. Shows steps 3 and 4.

81

Ribbons, which are available in a variety of widths, colors and materials add dimension, texture and movement to the landscape scene. Create movement and texture in the sky with ¼" wide ribbons. Allow the ribbon to wander through the sky and to cross over the border. Tack into place with French knots or beads. (See *Windowscape #1: Morning.*)

Ribbons may also be used to create three-dimensional roses, leaves and prairie points as shown in Illustration 5.4:

1. Cut the ribbon to form a rectangle at least 1 x 2 inches. To vary the sizes of the prairie points, cut several sizes of rectangles, always keeping the length twice as long as the width.

2. Fold down each corner to the midpoint on the bottom edge of the ribbon. Press. Insert prairie points into seams with either side of the prairie points face up.

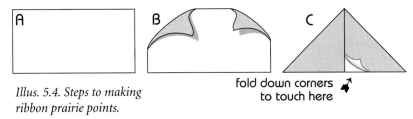

Illus. 5.4. Steps to making ribbon prairie points.

fold down corners to touch here

To make fabric prairie points follow these steps and refer to Illustration 5.5:

1. Cut a 3" square of fabric.

2. Fold fabric in half with the wrong sides together. Press. You now have a 1½" x 3" rectangle.

3. Fold down the top corners of the folded edge to the center of the raw edge. Press. Insert the prairie points into the seams with either side of the prairie points face up.

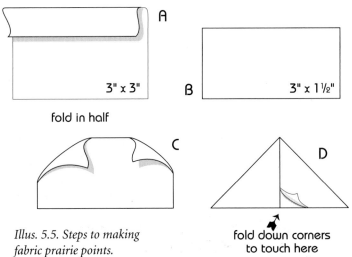

3" x 3"

fold in half

3" x 1½"

Illus. 5.5. Steps to making fabric prairie points.

fold down corners to touch here

82

To make ribbon or eyelet flowers and leaves follow these steps and see Illustrations 5.6 and 5.7:

1. Use ribbon or eyelet from ¼" to 1" wide.

2. Fold under and stitch the raw edge on one end of the ribbon/eyelet.

3. Take small running stitches along the edge. Gather the thread to form a small circle.

4. Overlap the raw edge with the finished edge and close.

5. For leaves: Cut ribbon at least 1" x 1½". Fold it to make a prairie point. With small running stitches, gather the bottom edge of the prairie point to create the leaf. Cut rectangles of various dimensions to vary leaf sizes.

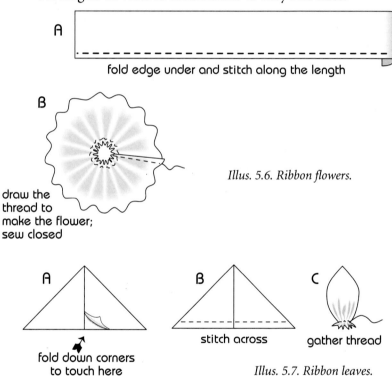

A
fold edge under and stitch along the length

B
draw the thread to make the flower; sew closed

Illus. 5.6. Ribbon flowers.

A
fold down corners to touch here

B
stitch across

C
gather thread

Illus. 5.7. Ribbon leaves.

Buttons come in all shapes, sizes and colors and add relief, texture and three dimensions to the landscape scene. Sew a button in the center of a flower or as an animal's eye; use the white buttons from blouses and shirts to depict baby's breath. Add sparkle to a nighttime sky or to the pebbles and stones on a rocky beach. Cluster the buttons so that they lie atop each other. Instead of using threads to tie a quilt, use buttons sewn on in a grid. Why not sew on the buttons with thread and leave the strands?

Beads and sequins also come in a wide variety of sizes, shapes, colors and finishes. Some are transparent; others are opaque.

Some are metallic or glass; others are wooden, ceramic or plastic. They add richness, light and a sense of movement to the landscape scene. Use beads to highlight a nighttime sky, or to make snow and rain glisten (See *Windowscape #4: The Storm*) and to depict the buttons on a dress or the pearls of a necklace.

Sew on a cluster of beads as the center of a flower or emphasize the outline of a flower with a row of seed beads. Combine different types of beads and sequins. When attaching beads to the quilt surface, it is advisable to use a beading needle and Nymo thread. The needle size should be larger than the bead size. For example, use a #13 needle with #12 beads. Beads are generally sewn on one at a time and a knot is tied after every third or fourth bead is attached. For a contemporary look, attach the sequins and beads to the surface with a drop of acrylic paint.

Many contemporary quilters are using acrylic paints and fabric markers instead of thread to embellish and to add textural interest to their surface designs. By painting splotches over all background fabrics, a disjointed background may be unified. Don't be afraid to get paint on the artifacts or on the thread. Every mark added to the quilt becomes a part of the whole. Paints may also be used to tone down or darken the color of a fabric to imply or to enhance the idea of distance in the landscape scene.

Do not apply oil-based paints which will deteriorate the fabric; use acrylic or other water-based paints such as Deka paints or fabric stenciling paints. Use the gloss acrylic gel as an extender; it makes the paint go further and if applied to the background fabric, it permits this background to show through the paints. Water may be added to the gel and to the paint in order to thin the paint so that it makes a wash. Mix the acrylic gel with glitter and apply as a wash over the background fabric. Attach sequins to the fabric with acrylic gel. The gel dries clear and will not add color behind the sequin. If color is desired behind the sequin, place the sequin onto a drop of acrylic paint.

Besides the acrylic paints, experiment with stick paints, puff paints, glitter paints and cold-water dyes. Cold-water dyes must be used on natural fibers such as cotton, linen, wool, silk and viscose rayon. To paint with the cold-water dyes, a dye thickening agent and fixative must be added.

Can there ever be too much embellishment? Personally, I say no! I love found objects, paint splotches and uncut threads. Set your imagination free! Exaggerate the three-dimensional aspect of your work and include your own symbolic treasures. Embellish on top of embellishment. Try painting the running stitches, outlining the reverse appliqué in paint or adding background writing in paint.

CHAPTER SIX

BORDER ELEMENTS

It is not imperative that a quilt have a border. The purpose of the border is to enclose and frame the quilt; to indicate the outer dimensions; to complement, strengthen, and complete the quilt; to give the viewer visual relief from the interior design; and to guide the viewer's eye back into the scene. Each quilt designer must decide whether a border complements or detracts from the interior design and whether to employ a border or not. There are myriads of antique and contemporary quilts alike that neither have nor need borders. When electing to use a border, it must become an extension of the interior design. The border, to be effective, must repeat lines, shapes, colors and patterns used in the interior design and must reinforce the theme of the interior design.

How many borders are needed to frame the scene? There is no wrong answer. I prefer to use at least two borders – one narrow and one wider. The inner, narrower border defines the outer dimensions of the scene and the outer, wider border frames the quilt and draws the viewer's eye back to the center. How wide should the borders be? Once again, there are no right or wrong widths. The border widths are not as crucial as are the proportions and the suitability of the borders to the interior scene. A border that is too wide overwhelms the scene; a border that is too narrow becomes insignificant; borders of equal width are monotonous and detract from the overall scene.

What type of border suits the landscape – pieced or appliquéd? Again, the choice is based on personal preference. Just as you collected photographs and pictures before designing the landscape scene, make a collection of photos which concentrate on border styles. Several sources of inspiration are children's books, calendars, wallpaper sample books, architectural motifs on buildings and existing landscape quilts. Ask yourself what you like and dislike about the borders; take notes on colors and motifs used and make sketches.

TRADITIONAL BORDERS

Borders may be whole cloth – whether a solid fabric or a printed border stripe – pieced or appliquéd. There are many options to the whole cloth border – from only one narrow border to five or six bands of varying widths. The most common whole cloth border is composed of an inner, narrow band, and an outer, wide band. A solid fabric whole cloth border frames the scene without detracting from it, complements the colors within the scene and provides space for elaborate machine or hand quilting. The corners (shown in Illustration 6.1) of a solid fabric border may be mitered, may include a corner square, or may use the butt joint.

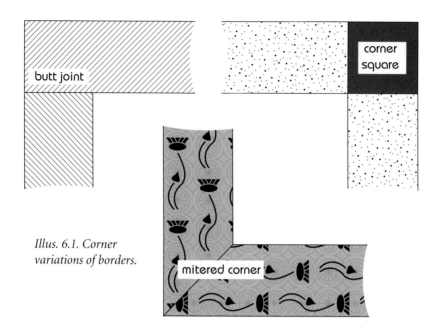

Illus. 6.1. Corner
variations of borders.

butt joint

corner square

mitered corner

The printed border stripe, formed of at least two coordinating printed stripes, should contain mitered corners so that the printed design flows smoothly around the corners. Because intricate quilting designs generally are not discernible on printed border striped fabrics, it is advisable to outline quilt the printed border motifs.

The second most common border style, found on many Amish quilts, is the border with corner squares. The border and corner squares may be composed of solid or printed fabrics that either complement or contrast to the interior design. To achieve a contemporary feel to the border, use plaid or stripe fabrics in the border and a solid in the corner squares. (See *Taxco.*) Another variation for this border style is to employ a pieced block instead of a plain block for the corner squares. One technique that I particularly prefer for this border style (shown in Illustration 6.2) is to appliqué flowers, leaves and vines in at least two of the corner squares.

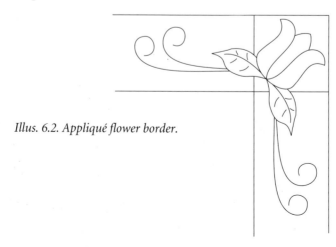

Illus. 6.2. Appliqué flower border.

The pieced border made of squares lends a folk art appearance to a landscape scene; is easy to design for square or rectangular quilts; does not detract from the landscape scene and easily repeats the fabric and colors employed within the scene. Pieced borders may highlight the colors and fabrics of the scene. The top border repeats the fabrics of the sky and clouds; the side borders highlight the sky fabrics and gradually intersperse the colors and fabrics of the mountains, trees, flowers, and grasses; and the bottom border reflects the colors and fabrics of the foreground.

The border made of squares is an excellent choice for novice landscape designers; it effectively frames the scene, turns the corner smoothly and repeats fabrics and colors. Try a border of squares for your first project, half-square triangles for a second quilt, and rectangles for a third project. See Illustration 6.3.

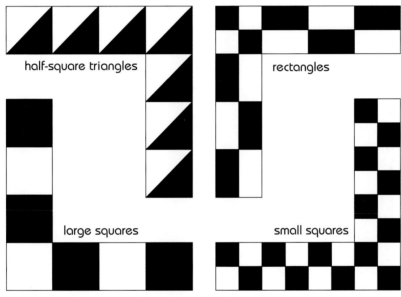

Illus. 6.3. Border alternatives.

The sawtooth border, Illustration 6.4a and 6.4b, is composed of squares made of half-square triangles, and is a popular pieced border in which the triangles are composed alternately of light and dark fabrics. It is a directional border which needs an even number of squares to turn the corners gracefully. In order to make a sawtooth border with an uneven number of squares turn the corner smoothly and have symmetrical corners, it may be necessary to reverse the direction of the triangles at the midpoint of the border strip. If you desire a formal, symmetrical sawtooth border, I recommend that you first design the border on graph paper in order to resolve the corners. If you prefer an informal border, it is not necessary to draft the border first. As with many antique quilts that contain sawtooth borders, you may simply end the borders without a resolution.

DIRECTIONAL BORDERS

Other directional borders, shown in Illustration 6.5, include the Reverse Sawtooth, the Double Sawtooth, Flying Geese, Chevrons, Folded Ribbons and Braided borders. In order to determine if it is necessary to reverse the direction of the blocks or only to reverse the direction of the colors, draft each border onto graph paper. Make multiple copies of the border. Experiment with colored pencils until you resolve the corners.

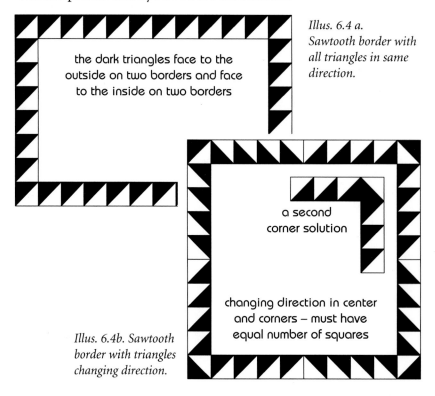

Illus. 6.4 a. Sawtooth border with all triangles in same direction.

the dark triangles face to the outside on two borders and face to the inside on two borders

a second corner solution

changing direction in center and corners – must have equal number of squares

Illus. 6.4b. Sawtooth border with triangles changing direction.

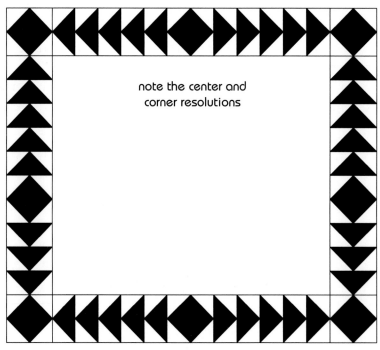

note the center and corner resolutions

Illus. 6.5. Flying Geese border.

One of my favorite techniques is to employ a pieced block in the border. The pieced block may be related to the landscape scene by title, theme or origin of design. Because I wanted the border frame of the quilt *Escurra* to depict a Spanish motif, I searched through books of Spanish and Moorish geometric designs and then drafted the chosen design into a 3" square. Due to the size limitations of these pieced block borders, it may be necessary (but not required) to keep the blocks simple. The following are a few suggestions for pieced block borders:

1. Hole in the Barn Door to frame a farm scene.

2. Keystones to frame a Pennsylvania scene.

3. Pine Trees or Tree Everlasting to frame a wooded scene.

4. Snowball to frame a winter scene.

5. Ohio Star, Pinwheels, Variable Star, Necker's Cube, Snowball and Nine-Patch.

If a block is too complicated, there are several options to pursue:

1. Eliminate some of the lines.

2. Use only a part of the block design.

3. Use the upper half of the block design for the top border, the lower half of the design for the bottom border, and the left and right halves of the block for the side borders.

Let's suppose that you have chosen a specific pieced border which does not fit the dimensions of your landscape scene. You may join this pieced border to the central panel by inserting a second border, whether a plain fabric or a floral border striped fabric, between the central design and the pieced border. The first step is to determine the size of the pieced border which most closely fits the interior or central design space. To determine the size of the plain or floral striped border needed:

1. Measure the length of the pieced border and the length of the landscape.

2. Subtract the length of the landscape scene from the length of the pieced border.

3. Divide the difference by two.

4. This number equals the width of the plain or floral striped border needed.

VERTICAL BARS BORDER

The vertical bars border continues the slant of lines from inside the quilt into the border. The bars may be of varied sizes and shapes. Simply extend the lines from inside the quilt into the border when drafting the cartoon. (See *Basque Fishing Village.*) If you do not wish to have the borders composed entirely of slant bars, construct a whole cloth border which is broken or interrupted by only a few diagonal lines. (Illustration 6.6.)

Illus. 6.6. Above left depicts a border of slant bars only. The example to the right depicts a few slant bars on a whole cloth border.

JAPANESE INFLUENCE

In the mid-1980's, due to the increased exchange of quilting ideas shared between the United States and Japan, a new border style emerged. Unlike the American preference for symmetrical borders, the Japanese prefer asymmetrical borders. There are no set rules concerning the number of bands, the border widths, color or fabric choice. For example, the top border may be 10" wide, the side borders 7" wide, and the bottom border 15" wide. The top and bottom borders may be two different colors with the sides a third color. The narrow band may either be at the top or the bottom and not on the sides. Refer to Illustration 6.7.

Illus. 6.7. Example of Japanese Scroll borders. The strips that compose these borders differ in size and color.

The composed or abstract border (as shown in Illustrations 6.8) is used by many of today's landscape quilt designers. Most often these borders are designed on the wall without prior planning on paper. Various fabrics are auditioned for the borders; that is, the fabrics are pinned next to the interior scene. If the fabrics go well with the scene, they are left pinned to the wall. More fabrics are auditioned. As some of the original fabrics are partially covered, new shapes appear. The process of making choices continues as new fabrics are auditioned and new shapes and patterns emerge.

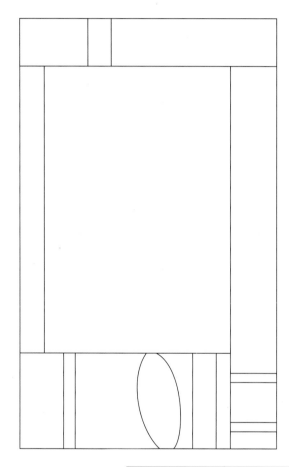

Illus. 6.8. Examples of composed or abstract borders.

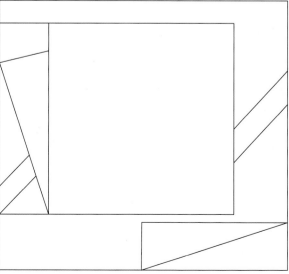

Quilt artist Ruth McDowell composes abstract borders which often contain design elements known as floats and "Spirit Lines" (Illustration 6.9). Floats are placed onto the quilt so that they cross both the border and the interior scene and carry previously used fabrics or colors into the border. To make floats, cut rectangles and bars in various dimensions, then place them on the border so that they appear to float between the border and the edge of the quilt. Appliqué into position. The composed border may contain "Spirit Lines". These are rectangles which have been pieced into the border to permit the quilt to breathe and to allow pieces of the sky to escape.

Illus. 6.9. Spirit Lines and Floats.

To this point, we have discussed structured borders which are pieced and which repeat fabrics from the central design area. There is also the visual border which suggests a border through change of color. The visual border, like the pieced border, defines the edge of the interior scene with a line. Unlike the pieced border, the visual border extends lines from within the interior scene into the border and completes the shape of the object in the border. For example, extend the lines of a pond, fence, tree branches or rocks beyond the border line. Complete the shape of these objects within the border space. Refer to Illustration 6.10.

Instead of repeating fabrics from the interior scene, change the palette of colors at the border. One method is to use the back of the fabrics. Try creating a visual border on three sides only – the top and the sides.

Illus. 6.10. Visual border.

The appliqué border is a decorative border which can easily be adjusted to fit any motif, border width or border length by simply adjusting the number or position of motifs, leaves and flowers. Many antique appliqué quilts did not possess appliqué borders that turned the corners gracefully. It was common to find vines that ran off at the border's edge, vines that only turned the corners symmetrically on two sides, and vines that differed on all four borders. The following folded paper techniques may be used to design symmetrical appliqué borders:

1. Cut paper border strips as long and as wide as the finished border. Fold the paper strips in half, then into fourths; continue to fold in half until units are a manageable size.

2. Measure the border length; divide the length by a number that yields divisions of equal lengths. Example: A border length of 75" may be divided into five sections, each 15" long. Cut out a paper strip 30" long, by the border width and fold in half. You now have a strip 15" long .

3. Sketch a running vine and flowers or an existing border design into one folded section.

4. Make adjustments in the spacing between flowers and leaves; add or subtract leaves and flowers.

5. Trace over the drawn lines with a black Sharpie® pen. Turn the folded strip over and trace the design onto the other side. Open to view the flow of the design.

6. To design a symmetrical corner square follow the steps below and refer to Illustration 6.11:

   a. Cut a paper square the size of the border corner.

   b. Fold the square in half diagonally.

   c. Tape the border strip to the corner square and mark the point where vines or corner pieces enter the corner square.

   d. Draw curves from these points to the diagonal line.

   e. Trace the curve on the other half of the square and a smooth, symmetrical corner has been created.

   f. Add leaves and flowers to complete the corner. Use the technique of tracing across the diagonal to make the corners symmetrical.

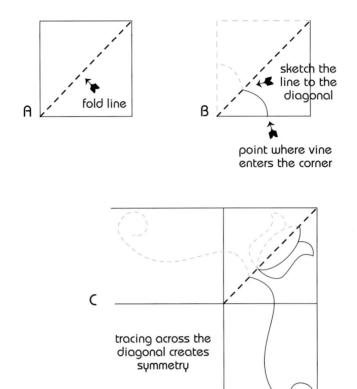

Illus. 6.11. Designing a symmetrical corner.

If the interrupted appliqué border and the symmetrical appliqué border do not suit your scene, think of the borders in various landscape terms (Illustration 6.12):

1. Above ground level, at ground level, and below ground level;

2. Sky, shoreline, ocean;

3. Sky, shoreline, beneath the ocean's surface;

4. Sky, background mountains, foreground fields.

In the landscape border, the top border may be composed of elements such as the sun, sun rays, the moon, phases of the moon, clouds, birds or the tips of tree branches. The side borders may be composed of pieced or appliquéd trees, plants and flowers or an appliquéd vine of flowers. The bottom border may be appliquéd with flowers, small animals, or insects; if it is a water scene, seashells, fish and coral would be appropriate.

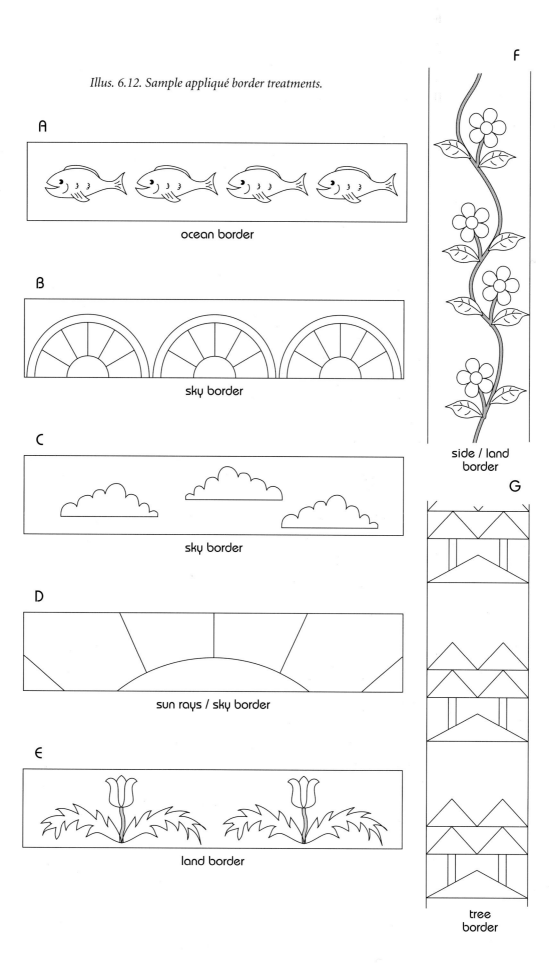

Illus. 6.12. Sample appliqué border treatments.

A

ocean border

B

sky border

C

sky border

D

sun rays / sky border

E

land border

F

side / land border

G

tree border

97

A second technique to creating a contemporary border is to "break" the border with a design element from the interior scene. For example, extend tree branches, fence posts, a garden path, a footbridge, or a small stream over the inner border strip into the outer border. By continuing the colors of the interior tree into the border, a more structured, formal border is created. If the colors of the tree branches change as they cross the border strips, a visual border is implied.

Although it is not essential to design each component of the borders during the drafting stage, it is imperative to plan the border as a part of the whole to determine the finished size of the quilt. Not every quilter resolves the questions of whether the borders will be straight-sided or shaped; patterned or plain; pieced, appliquéd or a combination of both techniques during the drafting stage. Step back from the quilt and let it tell you how to proceed. Sometimes it is necessary to put the quilt away for a few days or weeks, even a year, before the right solution presents itself. The borders have a sense of evolving by themselves; I've found that whenever I force a fabric or shape into the border, the quilt determines that it's wrong and another solution is required. Always let the quilt speak to you; take your time; leave the quilt on the wall and view it at various times of the day and night. Watch for the fabric or shape that jumps out at you and says, "I don't belong here." Also allow the quilt to determine its final shape, whether straight-edged or curved.

CHAPTER SEVEN

THE QUILTED LINE

After the quilt top has been completed, borders added and all embellishment worked, the quilting must be designed. The quilting lines secure the three layers of the quilt to make it more durable and create linear patterns across the quilt surface. More importantly, the quilting lines and linear patterns are visual, decorative marks that add texture to the quilt surface, enhance the dimension of depth, define and create shapes, and emphasize the subtle play of light and shadow.

The quilting lines of a landscape should reflect the natural elements found in nature. Use quilting lines to outline and to echo shapes such as ground contours; to fill in large spaces such as fields with furrows, mountains with crevasses, skies with wind streaks and cloud formations; and to depict details such as leaf veins and tree bark. Review the original idea source of your scene for tree lines, mountain crevasses, water currents, cloud formations, furrow patterns and cast shadows. Also examine photography books of landscapes, flowers and trees for quilting ideas. Before placing the quilting lines on the fabric, experiment drawing the quilting lines on the original cartoon, on tracing paper or on clear acetate that has been positioned on top of the cartoon. In this manner, different lines may be auditioned to see how they portray the natural forms.

Quilting lines may be straight or curved, broken or zig-zagged, parallel or intersecting, flowing or angular, closely or openly spaced. The contrast in choice of line and scale of line add visual texture and physical dimension to the scene. For example, parallel lines create a shadow between the two lines; closely quilted lines create intensity and flat surface which recedes into the distance; and sparsely quilted areas create calmness and a relief surface which moves forward visually. Dark areas of the landscape scene may be given more depth by quilting them heavily. Light areas of the scene seem to move forward when left free of quilting.

WIND STREAKS

There are two ways that the wind may be made discernible in a landscape scene. One is to appliqué objects in motion, such as a person leaning into the wind with his coattails and pants flapping, trees, flowers and grasses bending; or debris flying. The second way is to quilt the wind streaks into the finished piece. Quilted wind lines are parallel lines that need to be strategically placed – a group here, one over there, some close together, others further apart.

If there are snowflakes falling in the scene, the descent of the snowflakes will parallel the curved wind lines. Illustration 7.1, on page 102, demonstrates quilted wind lines.

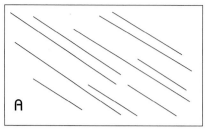

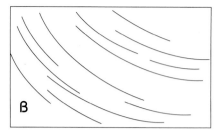

Illus. 7.1a. Wind Streaks.   *Illus. 7.1b. Wind and snow.*

CLOUDS

Clouds may be pieced, appliquéd or quilted into the sky. Quilted clouds must have soft curved edges. If the sky contains massive cloud formations, use the quilt line to divide the larger clouds into smaller areas and quilt little puffs into the corners of the big billows. Cloud streaks are quilted parallel to the horizon; remember to continue the cloud streaks behind all trees and mountain peaks. When quilting a moonlit scene, use quilt lines to portray the cloud streaks. If the ground is complex and angular, quilt the sky with wide, flowing lines. In order to intensify the brilliance of the sun, use grey quilting thread and place the quilt lines close together near the sun. Refer to drawings of cirrus, cumulus, stratus and nimbus clouds for accuracy. Illustration 7.2 demonstrates quilted cloud lines.

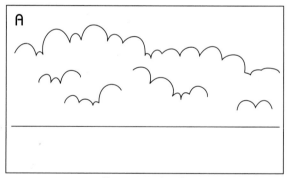

Illus. 7.2a. Clouds.

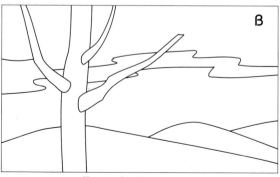

Illus. 7.2b. Cloud streaks.

102

The quilted line portrays the movement of water and its reflection in the landscape scene. All water, whether smooth or disturbed, has reflections and water streaks which may be quilted. Water streaks, crests and rolling waves in the foreground are larger and more widely spaced than those near the horizon. As the water streaks recede into the distance, the quilt lines come closer together. Remember to vary the size of the water crest and to quilt horizontal streak lines along the shore. Never quilt water lines in repeated arches. (Illustration 7.3a, b, c.)

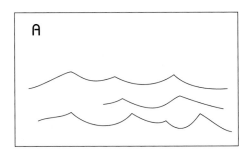

Illus. 7.3a. Water arches.

Illus. 7.3b. Water streaks.

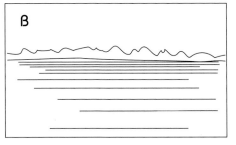

Illus. 7.3c. Water crescents.

Quilted lines may also be used to indicate a wet or flat, shiny surface. Quilt vertical lines in a puddle or pond to represent water streaks. Quilt one or two diagonal lines in the windowpane to represent glass streaks. (Illustration 7.4.)

Illus. 7.4a. Puddle surface.

Illus. 7.4b. Window surface.

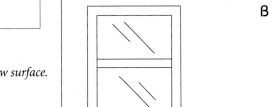

Quilted lines are also employed to indicate the movement of the water around and against rocks. To indicate movement of water around rocks, quilt water rings around the rocks. To portray a swift current that slaps against the rocks, quilt foam lines against the rocks. If the water is cascading, quilt parallel lines to suggest the descent of the water. Indicate the mist and foam at the bottom of the fall with soft, curved lines. (Illustration 7.5)

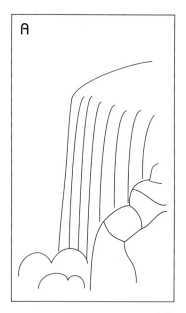

Illus. 7.5a. Waterfall.

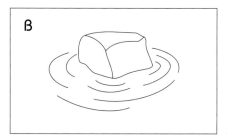

Illus. 7.5b. Rocks in the water.

TREES

Use the quilt line to give the tree bark its rough texture and to define the tree grooves. In large areas of greenery, outline tree limbs and give definition to individual leaf shapes or leaf clumps. Remember that tree limbs cross other limbs and that leaf clusters are in front of and behind the branches. Grass that is growing under the tree may be quilted in the shadow of the tree. (Illustration 7.6)

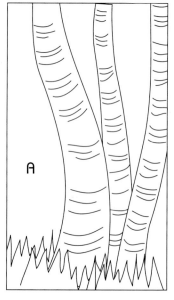

Illus. 7.6a. Tree bark.

Illus. 7.6b. Tree limbs.

Illus. 7.6c. Clumps of trees with trunks and limbs quilted.

Quilt rocky areas of the scene with angular lines to depict the planes of the rocks. In the shadows of the rock, quilt more closely to flatten the area and to enhance the perception of depth. Rocks appear harder if placed near soft forms such as clouds, sand, or water. Quilt the rocky areas with angular lines and the surrounding areas with flowing lines. When quilting a mountain range, vary the ridge and crevasse lines. Once again, quilt several crevasse lines close together to flatten the area and to give the visual appearance of depth. (Illustration 7.7)

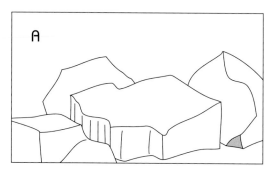

Illus. 7.7a. Rocks.

Illus. 7.7b. Mountain Ranges.

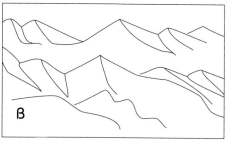

Quilt ground contour lines (Illustration 7.8) to add to the perception of depth. To depict a plowed field on gently rolling hills, indicate the furrows with curved quilted lines. The curved lines are spaced further apart in the foreground and closer together as the field recedes into the distance. For a flat field, quilt parallel lines and vary the pattern from field to field. For example, quilt lines one half inch apart and then leave a one inch space before the second set of parallel lines.

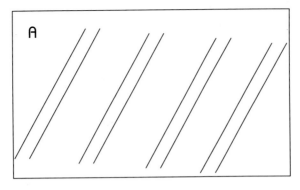

Illus. 7.8a.
Flat fields grid.

Illus. 7.8b.
Rolling fields.

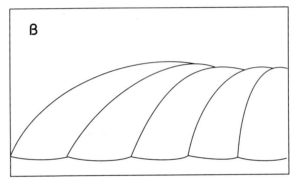

GRIDS

If you have used a floral design fabric for large grassy areas, quilt along the design motif. (See *Landscape: The Sheep.*) Geometric prints, plaids and striped fabrics provide ready made quilting patterns. Quilt in the spaces between the design motifs of a geometric print, or follow the printed lines of both plaids and striped fabrics to yield interesting grids. Large ground areas may also be filled with grids. Once again, experiment with various grids on the original cartoon. Refer to Illustration 7.9.

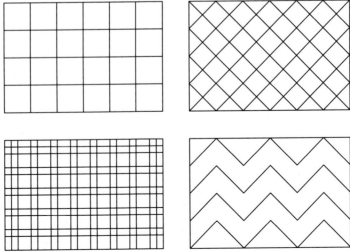

Illus. 7.9. Grids.

106

Hand quilters most often select a medium weight cotton thread such as #40 quilting thread. Cutting the thread no longer than 18" and running it through beeswax help to prevent tangling and fraying. The choice of thread color is determined by the fabrics and the personal preference of the quilter. Thread color may match or contrast with the fabrics and more than one color may be used. Thread that matches the fabric produces a smooth, unbroken line; thread that contrasts with the fabric emphasizes the individual stitches.

Both the size of the quilt needle (#7-12 betweens) and the thickness of the batt affect the size of the quilt stitch. Generally the thinner the batt and the smaller the needle, the smaller the quilt stitch is. Although hand quilters strive for small, evenly spaced stitches that produce smooth lines, larger, more bold quilt stitches can enhance the texture of and add dimension to areas of the landscape quilt. If you prefer to use a large quilt stitch, then emphasize the stitch by using pearle cotton, embroidery, buttonhole or metallic thread.

Use tying to embellish, to add a sense of dimension and to create grids by placing the ties across the quilt surface in a regular or an irregular pattern. Working with a variety of threads such as pearle cotton, embroidery or buttonhole thread, take a small stitch through all three layers and leave a tail of at least ½". Take a second stitch on top of the first stitch, tie a square knot and cut the threads so that both ends are of equal length. Continue in the same manner until an area is filled. If tying large areas of the quilt, cut a thread that is longer than the width of the area. Make two stitches in the first position but do not cut the thread. Continue to make the stitches across the width of the area. Midway between all double stitches, tie the threads and trim evenly.

When the appliqué is complete, trim all seam allowances to ¼" and press the quilt top. Mark all quilting lines onto the top with a quilt marking pencil. Cut the batt and the backing fabric at least 2" larger than the quilt top. Both the batt and the backing may be pieced. Because the batt has no grain or nap, it may be cut in any direction. Therefore, in order to join two batts together, cut pieces with straight edges, butt the edges and then sew with a loose herringbone stitch as shown in Illustration 7.10.

The one consideration to piecing the backing is the number of seams through which you must quilt. For the quilt, *Depth Charge #2: The Sea Dragons,* I wanted to use a special fabric that had been given to me for the backing. Since this fabric was not large enough even when pieced, I inserted sections cut from the "water" strips used in the background of the quilt top. By doing this I not only made the backing large enough, but created a unique back relevant to the top. To me, carrying the water theme to the quilt back outweighed quilting through extra seams.

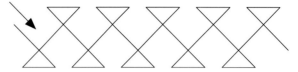

Illus. 7.10. Herringbone stitch.

BASTING THE QUILT TOP

Two or three days prior to basting together the three layers, open the quilt batt and spread it out flat on the floor. This permits the batt to breathe and the creases and folds to relax. Place the background fabric right side down onto a hard surface such as a wooden floor or table. Use masking tape to adhere the fabric; keep the fabric smooth and taut by taping opposite sides. Remove any stray threads from the backing fabric before placing the quilt batt bonded side up on top of the backing. Now center the landscape scene right side up onto the batt.

For small projects, safety pins may be used instead of basting. Always pin or baste from the center out so that all wrinkles are eased to the edges as shown in Illustration 7.11. When basting, thread two needles onto the basting thread and do not cut the thread from the spool. Using the first needle, baste from the center to the left side of the top; unwind thread from the spool as you sew. In the left seam allowance, knot the thread and remove the needle. The second needle still remains threaded on the spool. Unwind a length of thread from the spool that extends beyond the right side. Cut the thread and use the second needle to sew to the right.

When basting is completed, quilt the top by hand or machine. Hand quilting produces a soft line that sinks into the fabric while machine quilting produces a hard, well-defined line that remains on top of the fabric.

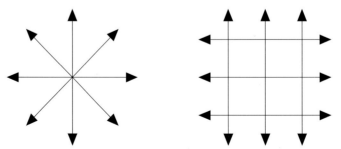

Illus. 7.11. Basting directions.

Recommended Reading

Blake, Wendon. *Landscapes in Oil.* New York: Watson-Guptill Publications, 1979.

Brouillette, Al. *The Evolving Picture.* New York: Watson-Guptill Publications, 1987.

Carlson, John F. *Carlson's Guide to Landscape Painting.* New York: Sterling, 1953.

Denton, Susan and Barbara Macey. *Quiltmaking.* New York: Sterling Publishing Co., Inc., 1987.

Horton, Roberta, *Plaids & Stripes.* Lafayette, CA: C & T Publishing, 1990.

James, Michael. *The Second Quiltmakers Handbook.* Englewood Cliffs: Prentice Hall, Inc., 1981.

Johnson, Cathy. *Drawing & Painting from Nature.* New York: Design Press, 1989.

McDowell, Ruth B. *Pattern on Pattern.* San Francisco: The Quilt Digest Press, 1991.

Marston, Gwen & Joe Cunningham. "Appliqué Borders", Issue #13, *Ladies Circle Patchwork Quilts.* New York: Lopez Publications. May/June, 1989.

Martin, Judy. *Patchworkbook.* New York: Charles Scribner's Sons, 1983.

Montano, Judith. *The Crazy Quilt Handbook.* Lafayette, CA: C & T Publishing, 1986.

Paramon, Jim. *Perspective.* Tucson, AZ: HP Books, 1982.

Penders, Mary Coyne. *Color and Cloth.* San Francisco: The Quilt Digest Press, 1989.

Rines, Frank M. *Landscape Drawing with Pencil.* New York: Van Nostrand Reinhold Co., 1984.

Sienkiewicz, Elly. *Baltimore Beauties and Beyond, Volume I.* Lafayette, CA: C & T Publishing, 1989.

Wells, Jean. *A Patchworthy Apparel Book.* Atlanta: A Yours Truly Publication, 1981.

Wignall, Jeff. *Landscape Photography.* New York: Michigan Hall Book Co., 1987.

About the Author

Sheryl Morrow Robinson began quilting in 1973 to make baby quilts for her nephews. Her quilt teaching career began in 1981. She lectures and teaches appliqué and color study classes throughout the Pittsburgh area where she resides with her husband, Alan, and son, Elliott. Sheryl is also a member of the Fiberarts Guild, the North Pittsburgh Quilter's Guild and Quilter's Triangle. She has exhibited in the local galleries and has held several one-woman shows in the area. Sheryl's quilts are in both private and public collections.

Other books from Boyd Publishing:

Taking Off With Flying Geese, Johnson, $14.95.

Frogs and Flowers:Impressions of Ponds & Gardens Made into Quilts, Remme, $17.95.

So, Mrs. Smith, You Say You're 35 and You Still Like to Play With Blocks, Shimp, $17.95.

Patterns from Boyd Publishing:

Alphabet Sampler Quilt, Huey, $5.50.

Indian Paintbrush, Ludwig, $5.50.

Circle of Points Tree Skirt, Riddle, $5.50.

Coming Soon:

Modular Magic:Module Designs for Unique Quilts, Remme, 1992.

Heaven's Above, Stangness, 1992.